BEYOND
THE SHAME

One Mother's Journey to Healing
in Front of the Bars

Published and distributed in Canada and the United States by: Ahava Chai – an imprint of LOVE + Lifestyle Publishing Group, Inc. www.lovelifestylepublishing.com • Published and distributed in United Kingdom by: Ahava Chai UK – an imprint of LOVE + Lifestyle Publishing Group UK , Ltd. • Published and distributed in Australia by: Ahava Chai Australia – an imprint of LOVE + Lifestyle Publishing Group Australia Pty. Ltd. • Published and distributed in the Republic of South Africa by: Ahava Chai SA – an imprint of LOVE + Lifestyle Publishing Group SA, Pty. Ltd. • Published and distributed in India by: Ahava Chai India – an imprint of LOVE + Lifestyle Publishing Group India:

All associated logos are trademarks and/or registered trademarks of LOVE + Lifestyle

Publishing Group. www.lovelifestylepublishing.com

Cover Design by: Ahava House Media Group Interior

Design by: Ahava House Media Group All rights reserved.

Publisher Prefix: 978-1-77210

Hardcover ISBN: 978-1-77210-046-4

Paperback ISBN: 978-1-77210-047-1

Ebook ISBN: 978-1-77210-048-8

Ahava Chai, September 2016

Printed in the United States of America.

Dedication

To my three amazing children who,
through their individual journeys,
forced me onto a path of discovery, growth and self-healing.

To truly move forward, one must count their many blessings, pull oneself out from under the weight of self-doubt, guilt and shame and embrace the lessons learned as a roadmap to unbelievable triumph.

Introduction

Every mother wants the best for her children and wants to believe that she can protect them from anyone or anything that may want to harm them. I've finally realized that we can only protect and teach them so much.

We can teach them to look both ways before crossing the road. To not touch the stove when it's hot and to treat others as they would like to be treated, among other great life lessons. Then we have to let them go and hope that they always make the right choices and become amazing human beings who make the world a better place or at the very least to learn from their mistakes and take responsibility for their actions.

So when our children, regardless of age, become involved in the justice system, it's only natural to blame ourselves and to feel that we failed them somewhere along the way. This is a long and painful journey. The truth is, we did not fail. We were unprepared for the strength of the negative pull they face every day and the difficult choices they would face on a daily basis. We were unprepared to accept the fact that they would eventually become independent people on which we were not the only influence. That friends, media and other adults who come into their lives would ultimately influence their thoughts, beliefs and actions.

Often experiencing overwhelming guilt and feelings of shame, isolation, loneliness and hopelessness amongst many other emotions as a direct result of a loved one's involvement in the justice system, we become the unseen victims of circumstance. We are forced to embark on a journey which teaches us to accept our limitations, to draw from the strengths within and around us and to first and foremost take care of our emotional, spiritual and physical health. *Beyond the Shame* is an understanding and strength that we only discover through this journey. Ultimately, we discover that by drawing on the undiscovered strength within and from those also on that path we can do great things.

I struggled to answer the questions: Where did I go wrong? What could I have done differently? among many others. The answers continually elude me.

How could someone like me go so terribly wrong, not once but twice? Someone, who considered themselves to have strong moral values, a healthy respect for the law and an unwavering commitment to raising her children with the same belief system. Someone, who dedicated her life to working with adults and teens whose lives had taken a wrong turn and landed them in conflict with the law. Why couldn't I have prevented my own children from walking on the wrong side of it?

Somehow, I naively thought that I would be exempted from having to travel down that road with my own children. That my respect for the law and strong moral compass would be inherited by them, much like my brown eyes. Never could I have imagined that this would not be the case.

For the most part, I was "raised right" in a two parent home. My father was a strict, somewhat over-bearing man and my mother a hard-working woman both of West Indian heritage. They instilled in us a strong sense of right and wrong and the value of the truth.

Oh, don't get me wrong, I got myself in my fair share of mischief as a child and tested my parents' patience with my strong personality. I was independent to a fault. Some would say stubborn, but I still had a healthy fear of my father and the law.

Can I truly find the answers that would wipe away the paralyzing guilt and shame I feel?

For over 15 years I have searched diligently for an answer, something that would help me move Beyond the Shame and release me from underneath the unbearable weight of failure.

Maybe the answers I seek are not in my present but in the past. So I travel back, back to the events that changed my life forever.

Who am I?

To know where you're going you need
only to know where you're from.

Who am I? Now that's a loaded question, as who we are tends to change over the years. New people come in and out of our lives leaving their imprint, good and bad, life experiences, choice of partners, children and even careers impact who we truly are. So let's start with the basics. The rest you can decide for yourself at the end of our journey.

I was born on January 6, 1964, in a small private hospital in Manchester England. Weighing in at 8 lbs 6 oz., reportedly, a healthy, beautiful baby girl to hard-working middle-class parents. My mother a nurse and my father a mechanic with an army background.

I migrated from England to Ontario, Canada in May of 1972 and settled into a modest apartment in Toronto with my parents, two older sisters and one older brother. A younger sister would suddenly appear in my life from Jamaica later along the way.

My father was an extremely strict man who ruled his family with an iron fist and had a multitude of rules and expectations for his children. Children were to be seen and not heard, speak only when spoken to and answer when called, the first time. He was a disciplinarian who believed in corporal punishment and used it liberally to control our behaviour. By today's standards, some would say he was emotionally and physically abusive, but by West Indian standards, this was the norm. I attribute this to my strong sense of right and wrong, but also to the overwhelming sense of fear and anger I often feel when challenged or controlled.

My mother was a somewhat docile woman of small stature who worked hard to contribute to the household. I can only imagine that the financial responsibility of raising five children with limited choices, was extensive and with that I try to understand her absence. I don't remember much of my mother's parenting style as she worked afternoons and was away from the home at times when most children were home from school. My older sister, Sharon played the primary caregiver role in my life at that time.

As children, we were not permitted to leave the house or play with our friends after certain hours. We were not permitted to stay or eat at any other home than our own. Bedtime was 6:00pm and was strictly enforced. Later bedtimes were earned as we grew older. To tell you the truth, I'm not sure if it was because my parents strongly believed that children required a great amount of sleep in order to promote development, if they just needed time to themselves or if it was just another way to control us.

We were responsible for preparing meals and general upkeep of the home. On Saturdays the girls were responsible for major cleaning where the entire house had to be cleaned from top to bottom, followed by an inspection before we were permitted to go out with our friends. Sunday was family day which meant no going outside or having friends come over, a large family dinner at 2:00pm sharp and attending Sunday School. Although this is a practice I lost along the way, it gave me a foundation in faith that I would come to rely on later in my life.

Given what seemed like a never-ending list of unfair rules and restrictions, we all become individuals who sought our independence at an early age. Most of us leaving home shortly after the age of eighteen. Some of our own volition and others due to what my parents viewed as unacceptable behaviour.

I fell second to the youngest in the family line and had a fairly good relationship with my siblings, some closer than others. By all accounts, I had a fairly good childhood despite what I viewed as a form of incarceration full of rules and restrictions. I grew to be a strong-willed young lady with somewhat of a rebel streak. Yes. I was stubborn and determined to do things my way and on my own terms. Little did I know where my stubbornness would lead me.

Shock and Disbelief

When offered a blessing, ask not why,
embrace the opportunity and run
with it.

A brisk December morning in 1984. As usual, I was on the move, this time trying to catch the bus that would take me to work for another fun filled day in the retail world. Not really my dream come true, but at that time I had not yet decided what I wanted to do with my life, so it served its purpose of providing me with an income that afforded me the means to live a healthy social life.

As I stood patiently awaiting the arrival of my only mode of transportation, I felt the wind slap me across the face like a branch slamming against the window in a wind storm. It's cold, if I had to guess, I would say about -10 degrees Celsius. Typical for a stubborn soul like mine, this was not something I considered when I left the house that morning as my choice of outerwear was very inappropriate for the cold. So I stood there shaking like a leaf as the flaps of my dark brown bomber jacket blew to either side of my body exposing my navy blue sweater that almost matched my blue jeans which laid close onto my legs. Of course, I was way too cool to zip it up. My fingers were numb and my socks and toes soaked through my white and black Adidas running shoes.

In the distance, I could see the big white bus with the orange stripe on the side slowly approaching as it plowed through the snow covering the road. Thank God because I had been feeling a little under the weather for the past few days and didn't think I could stand out there a minute longer.

I stepped towards the curb as I anticipated boarding the bus, where surely it would be much warmer than where I stood for the last ten minutes, only to be pushed aside by a tall, well dressed gentleman in a long black wool coat that almost fully covered his grey dress pants. On his feet he wore these rubber shoe covers over his expensive looking shiny black shoes. I only remember this because I thought it looked ridiculous. Obviously, he needed to get to his destination before I did and that one extra step in front of me would ensure that that happened.

As the bus drew near, I was relieved to see that it wasn't too crowded and thought that I may actually get a seat, preferably one by the window where I could rest my wet feet on the heater. The bus came to a stop about three feet to my left, forcing me to walk through a nice puddle of slush in my already soaked running shoes. I turned to my left and followed my impatient friend in the wool coat and now two others who just happened to be standing directly in front of where the open bus door now rested.

I approached the opened door which revealed a stocky fellow with curly brown hair slightly balding on the top seated in a tattered looking leather seat behind the steering wheel. His uniform appeared freshly pressed and his boots black and shiny. He glanced over from his seat as I boarded the bus, not saying anything at all. I placed my coins into the tall metal and glass box situated between his tattered seat and myself. I listened for the clanging sound the coins make when they drop down into the container and looked to make sure that I had paid the correct amount. I then began to make my way to the last empty seat on the bus near the back rear exit door. I always sat near the rear door just in case anything happened, I could get off fast. I quickly realized that my well-dressed friend was again ahead of me. What were the chances that he would let me have the last seat? You guessed it, none!

I approached the middle of the bus and placed the long shoulder strap of my black pleather purse over my left shoulder, clasped it with my left hand holding it close to my body and took hold of the metal support pole with my right hand. I was now settled in for the thirty or so minute bus ride to the subway station. So much for the warm window seat with the heater.

Several minutes into the ride I was overcome by a warm sensation which seemed to travel through my body and up into my head. Then, fade to black!

"Are you ok? Are you ok?" A faint voice whispered. I awakened to the stalky, slightly balding bus driver with the curly brown hair standing over me repeating, are you ok? As the fog in my head and the glaze over my eyes cleared, I responded, "Yes. I, just wasn't feeling well. What happened?" "I think you fainted." He quickly responded, with a slight hint of concern in his voice. He then stretched out his right hand to help me to my feet. The faint smile on his face made him appear concerned and genuine. I took his hand as a slight build woman with dirty blond shoulder length hair, dirty blue Levi jeans, worn out Puma running shoes and an old brown leather coat rose from her seat near the front of the bus and helped me into it. The large dark bags under her eyes, dry skin on her face and slightly greying temples made her appeared much older than I'm sure she was but her smile was friendly and comforting.

The bus driver repeatedly checked in with me to ensure that I was doing ok as he drove. I'm sure that part of his concern came from his fear that something else would happen to me resulting in him being held responsible for not reporting my earlier fainting incident. I felt fine, a little tired, but that was nothing new. As much as he insisted, I wasn't about to go to waste my entire day in Emergency only to be told something I already knew, I was fine.

The remainder of my bus ride was uneventful, if you don't count the endless stream of teenagers who couldn't resist pulling the plastic coated cord above the windows which tells the bus driver that you want to get off at the next stop. They must have gotten a kick out of it because the majority of the time, none of them got off when the bus stopped. I could tell that the bus driver was not impressed with their behaviour, but he kept it to himself only glancing back at them with a look of frustration and disappointment on his face.

Finally, my stop, Islington Subway Station. I rushed off the bus because I was already late for work and still had to get on the subway to Dundas West Station. Surprisingly, I felt pumped, not like you'd expect someone who supposedly passed out on the bus to feel.

As usual, the subway station was crowded with people from all walks of life, all of them rushing somewhere, pushing each other as they tried to squeeze onto the train before it pulled away. Me, I wasn't about to risk life and limb for $3.75/hr. So I watched as the first train pulled out of the station and headed down the dark tunnel. I really couldn't understand what the urgency was because another train came rushing into the tunnel about two minutes later. After all, it was rush hour.

About ten minutes to the Crossways at Dundas and Bloor, I thought to myself. That should be just enough time to figure out what I was going to tell my boss, John. Oh, what the hell, the truth never killed anyone so I opted for the truth. That way I wouldn't have to remember the lie later on down the road.

By the time the train arrived at Dundas West Station, I was already thirty minutes late for work. Good thing the store was just across the street from the station. I took off like a bat out of hell flying through the subway station like OJ through the airport, exited the station, dashed across the street against the light, I must add, and in through plaza doors.

In no time I was rushing into the store, hoping that no one would notice that I was late. You know that's the time when your boss just happens to be at the front door right? Well, true to form, there John stood to my left counting the till with Anita, the senior cashier. I quickly apologized for being late and ran into the back room to take off my jacket and grab my blue pinney, John's version of a uniform.

I immediately returned to the floor and explained to John what had happened on the bus and went straight to folding the mess of clothing that was left from last night's shift. I really hate when customers pick stuff up and then without thought just throw them back in a big pile. You know the ones? They're convinced that the best shirt is the one at the bottom of the pile, but still have to pick up every shirt, unfold it and have a look before dumping it carelessly back on the shelf.

About an hour passed when suddenly I began to feel light headed again. I grabbed onto the upper shelving to support myself when I saw Hilda come rushing over to make sure that I was alright. She was a little Italian woman standing about 5' tall, stocky build, salt and pepper hair and a strong Italian accent. "You don't look too good," she said with her strong accent. She grabbed the small metal step ladder that was leaning up against a nearby wall and instructed me to take a seat. "I'll be right back," she said before disappearing down the aisle leaving me perched on the ladder awaiting her return. "Ok now let's go get you checked out." She said as she approached me with John directly behind her. He had this worried look on his face as he walked towards me asking if I was going to be ok. I removed my pinney and handed it to him as he helped me to my feet. Hilda and I left the store with her holding me tightly as if she feared that I would pass out before we reached her car. During our walk to the car, she couldn't resist her mothering instinct as she began to ask me a series of questions about my health and how I was feeling. We exited the building and into her car that she had already brought to the front. I guess that was what she had done when she left me seated on the step ladder, and off we went.

After a short ride to St Joseph's Hospital, we entered through the double doors leading into the Emergency area where I was overwhelmed by the smell. A combination of antiseptic and various bodily odors lingered in the air. That warm sensation again began to creep up my body as I braced myself against the nurses' station.

An older looking woman with a chocolate brown complexion, jet black hair pulled back in a tight ponytail propped on top of her head wearing a light blue nurses uniform stood up from behind the desk. "How can I help you today?" she asked. "I don't feel well and I apparently fainted on the bus earlier today," I told her. She then asked me to sit in the chair which was to the right of her desk. I remember looking at it, an old worn out plastic thing that looked as though it had seen better days. She picked up her white plastic clipboard which had a white piece of paper on it and her pen as she swung her chair around to face me. She immediately began to ask me a barrage of questions and diligently jotted down my answers on the piece of paper which, to be honest, annoyed me to no end. All I wanted to know was what was wrong with me.

After taking my temperature, blood pressure and health card information, she asked me to sit in the waiting room located to my left until I was called in to see the doctor. I slowly made my way to the seating area and sat on the chair on the end next to Hilda, picked up a National Geographic magazine and began to flip through the pages.

I sat patiently flipping through the magazine, looking at the pictures as my mind raced thinking of all the things that could be wrong with me. It seemed like hours had passed before I heard a frail voice call out my name. "Miss Murdock." I sprung to my feet, threw the magazine back onto the table and headed towards the voice, leaving Hilda behind, as now I felt that I was going to throw up. "Follow me," she said. She was a large woman, at least 5' 11" tall and well over 200lbs. She wore a white nurse's uniform, which looked clean and freshly pressed, but to be honest, a little snug and short for a woman her size and age. Her voice was now strong and commanding but she smiled when she spoke which took the edge off, I guess.

I followed her through a set of brown, windowed double doors into an area with an even stronger odor, tons of people milling around and several others lying on beds inside small cubicles sporting multi-coloured curtains; for privacy, I suppose. She escorted me into the first cubicle we approached on the right and handed me a small plastic bottle with a bright orange lid and asked me to provide a urine sample after she took some blood in order to run a few tests. She then scurried out of the cubicle drawing the multi-coloured curtain behind her.

I got down off the bed and peeked my head out from behind the curtain into the hallway. To my right at the end of a short hall I could see the sign for the washroom. I exited the cubicle with the plastic bottle tightly concealed in my right hand so no one could see what I was about to do. The washroom was small and had a strong odor of bleach or some other kind of cleaner. The smell did nothing to help my nausea. I sat on the toilet seat still trying to think what on earth could have been wrong with me. I hadn't eaten anything yet that morning so it couldn't be food poisoning, I thought. I sat there for what seemed like forever waiting to fill that stupid plastic bottle. Of course, nothing came and the nurse knocking on the door only made me feel rushed, which seemed to stall the process even more. After a few more minutes, I finally completed the task, sealed the bottle, wrapped it in a paper towel and exited the washroom as quickly as I entered.

I returned to the cubicle with the plastic bottle, now warm with my urine, carefully wrapped in a paper towel and placed it on the small metal tray which was sitting on the little table beside the bed.

"Miss. Murdock," she called out as she bursts through the multi-coloured curtains surrounding my cubicle, pushing a two shelf metal cart with two plastic bins. "I need to take some blood. Did you get the sample?" She casually asked. Mortified by her casual tone, I simply pointed to the small table where I had just placed the plastic bottle. She picked up the bottle, pulled a pen from her left front pocket and wrote on the bottle, my name I guess and then carefully placed it in the top bin on the cart. She then removed a small white packet containing an alcohol pad from one of the plastic bins. "Roll up your sweater sleeve," she said. Not much bedside manner with this one, I thought. I complied by pulling up the sleeve of my left arm, exposing my bare arm up to just above the mid-bicep. "Make a fist," she instructed. I complied. Without hesitation, she tied a large rubber tourniquet around my arm just above my elbow, removed the alcohol pad from the package and began to rub it up and down against the inner part of my elbow. Before I could blink, in went the tiny needle attached to a thin rubber tube. She took her left hand and removed a small glass vial from the table while tightly holding onto the contraption now sticking out of my arm and attached it to the tube. With a snap she removed the tourniquet and the small glass vial began to quickly fill with my blood as if it was being sucked right out without permission. First one vial and then another and another. Hope she leaves me some, I thought.

After placing the final vial of blood on the table, she slowly removed the needle from my arm and applied a small band aid over the injection site and with a, "now that wasn't too bad," she exited the cubicle, this time using her right hand to swing the multi-coloured curtains closed behind her.

I sat waiting on the not-so-comfortable bed staring at the charts and gadgets hanging on the walls thinking: this place is a little on the morbid side; no wonder people are sick in here.

Again the multi-coloured curtains open with the thrust of a hand but this time a well-polished looking gentleman, standing about 5' 7", piercing grey eyes with dark rimmed glasses, short sandy brown hair and a tanned complexion entered the room wearing a white lab coat with a shiny silver and black stethoscope hanging loosely around his neck, black dress pants and black loafers. His name tag read "Dr. Samuels."

"Miss Murdock? My name is Dr. Samuels, I understand that you fainted earlier today and that you haven't been feeling quite like yourself lately." "Yes." I responded. "Well, I think I may be able to explain why," he said. He continued to say, "your urine sample shows that you're pregnant. We will confirm with a blood test, but that explains what has been happening to you."

I didn't hear another word that came out of his mouth although I could see his lips moving. All I could think was: He must be mistaken. Not me! Not now! Daddy is going to kill me. Tears of fear welled up in my eyes and slowly began to run down my cheeks. The taste of salt made me nauseous as the tears ran into my mouth. Dr. Samuels said something else which sounded like gibberish to me and then exited the cubicle leaving me in a puddled mess slouched over on the cold, uncomfortable bed.

As I tried to regain my composure, the tall nurse with the commanding voice entered the cubicle. With a soft tone, as soft as is possible for her I think, she asked "are you ok? By your reaction, I take it that this is not the news you were hoping for."

"No shit, Sherlock!"

"Is there someone I can call for you?" I could only shake my head no as I was still overwhelmed with shock and disbelief. "Can I call the baby's father?" she asked. Again I could only shake my head. All I wanted was for her to say that I was not pregnant after all, but that never came out of her mouth. Instead she proceeded to tell me that the blood test confirmed the pregnancy and that it looked like I was due in early August. She continued to tell me to ensure that I went to see my family doctor as soon as possible to start my prenatal care. She then left the room after briefly holding my hand and wishing me well. This time leaving the curtain open. I guess that was my cue to leave.

Now, what? How do I go home? How long can I hide this pregnancy before people start to notice? I don't want to be a mother! Not now. Not like this. I thought I had this part of my life all planned. I would not have any kids until I was married and have a career. So, do I go through with this? Do I have this baby? I felt as though my head would explode with all the questions flying through it.

I pulled myself together enough to get up off the bed, gather my belongings and head back to the waiting room where Hilda still sat on the uncomfortable little chairs. As I approached, she sprang to her feet with that motherly look of concern on her face. I assured her that I was physically fine and then shared what the doctor had just told me. She held me as if to console me, but that only brought back the tears.

Hilda drove me back to the subway station and offered to let John know that I would not be back at work that day.

I spent the next few hours riding the public transit in a trance, flip-flopping between bouts of anger and uncontrollable sobbing. How could I have been so stupid? I'm twenty years old and have no idea what I want to do with my life and now I'm expected to raise another human being.

Of course, the first person I told was my best friend Patricia and a few days later, I reluctantly told Cliff that he was going to be a father. Cliff and I had met while in high school and along with three other friends became somewhat inseparable as we shared a common interest in music. We weren't in what you would characterize as a committed relationship at that time and his parents were less than pleased with our relationship and now his pending fatherhood. Despite everyone's conviction that we would fail and the fact that neither of us had planned for this so soon in our lives, we also knew that all things happened for a reason and who were we to question God's plan. That day we decided that we would have this child and raise him/her together.

A few weeks later I gathered the courage to tell my parents and as expected I was asked to leave the family home. Desperate and alone, I called my best friend Patricia whose family then graciously offered to give me a place to stay while I figured out my next move.

For the first few months, Cliff was attentive as we tried to build a relationship that would stand the test of parenthood and he had even given me a ring as a sign of his commitment to our relationship. In the Spring of 1985, halfway through my pregnancy all that changed when, in the middle of the night, I received a call from a woman who questioned me about my rumored pregnancy, the fact that Cliff was the father and informed me that she was also in a relationship with Cliff and had just received a ring from him solidifying their relationship.

To say that I was devastated would be an understatement. Here I was now about to bring a child into the world alone. I was overcome with anger and I vowed that no matter what, I would raise the perfect child alone. He/she would want for nothing and I would do whatever it took to ensure that he/she grew to be a strong, independent, well-adjusted young person. The relationship between Cliff and I ended that day along with any expectation that he would help me raise our child.

Single Motherhood

Sometimes only through great struggle
does true clarity raise its head.

Let me say, giving birth DOES NOT make you a mother any more than flying on an airplane makes you a pilot. The title is earned along the way as you learn to give selflessly, to sacrifice your dreams and self for the benefit of another, to love unconditionally without wanting, acquire and apply the many other skills needed to raise a well-adjusted individual who can confidently go out and build a life of their own and become positive contributor to making the world a better place. This is no easy feat.

"There is no way to be a perfect mother…. but a million ways to be a good one."

Unknown Author

A Mother is defined as:

Someone that gives rise to or exercises protecting care over someone else.

Dictionary.com

The woman who loves you unconditionally from birth, the one who puts her kids before herself and the one who you can always count on above everyone else.

Urban Dictionary.com

At the age of twenty-one, my views on parenting were what I would call 'oppositional'. I was determined to do the exact opposite of what I thought my parents had done. I would......

- Never physically discipline my children
- Allow them to make their own choices and have input into decisions which affected them
- Encourage them to speak freely
- Ensure that they always knew that they can come to me with anything, no matter how bad
- Raise them with unconditional love, not with fear

Even armed with this knowledge and intent, I was less than prepared for what motherhood would bring my way.

Saturday, August 3, 1985, began like any other Caribana Saturday. I got up, spoke with Patricia on the phone to confirm our plan for the day's events. It would start with a trip on the Go Train from Mississauga to Toronto to enjoy the Caribana parade followed by a jam at whichever club Kilowatts Sound Crew was playing, just like we had done many years in the past. This time was a little different however, as I was very pregnant and due any day. Despite everyone's insistence that I stay home and rest, I got myself dressed and off we went. No, it wasn't just my stubbornness. To tell you the truth, I was terrified that I would go into labour and be alone as everyone was going to be at the parade.

As always the parade was filled with elaborate costumes, imaginative floats, steel bands on the back of trucks, lots of great music and hundreds if not thousands of people from various cultures enjoying themselves. Patricia and I were no exception as we followed the various floats along University Avenue. That was until I began to show signs of discomfort and decided to go home to get some rest.

Later that night I was awakened by the extremely uncomfortable feeling of a rock hard stomach. This really wasn't anything new except this time no matter what I did, that baby would not move to ease my discomfort. After a few minutes I began to panic because just as I feared, everyone I knew was still at the Caribana festivities. I went back to bed hoping that it would ease but a few hours later I was again awakened by the same feeling. It was now morning and it was clear that something was going on with this baby. I picked up the phone and called Dr. Franklin and informed him of the events of the past few hours. He instructed me to get to the hospital as soon as I could. I tried calling Patricia and reluctantly Cliff to no avail so with no other choice, I reached out to my cousin Anna who agreed to take me to the hospital.

At 2:10pm on August 4th. I gave birth to Jermaine, my handsome little prince alone in a hospital room at St. Joseph's Hospital in Toronto after a fairly uneventful delivery.

He was perfect! Ten fingers, ten toes, a full head of straight black hair and the chubbiest cheeks I have ever seen. Truly a blessing, in a life not yet lived.

As I held this little bundle of joy in my arms for the first time, I realized how truly alone I was in the world. My parents had thrown me out of the house when they learned of the pregnancy. In true stubborn fashion, it would be several years before I spoke to or saw them again. I had lost touch with my siblings as they were living their own lives, raising families and building careers. My shame and disappointment of being an unwed mother, took care of most of my friendships as I withdrew from everyone. From that day forward it was my prince and I against the world.

The next six days were spent in the hospital where I was given a crash course on how to take care of my little miracle. Armed with as much knowledge as one could acquire in six days and while still recovering from major body trauma (giving birth is not easy on the body) it was time for me to leave the safety of the hospital. It was now time to begin building a life, not just for myself but for my prince as well. I was terrified! Babies didn't come with directions nor motherhood with a manual, but somehow I was going to have to finish raising myself and raise this incredible human being.

The first time I heard that scream in the middle of the night that sent me flying out of my bed and into the air with a look of total terror and confusion on my very tired face was just the beginning. It was clear then that my life was forever changed and nothing would ever be the same. Everything from that day forward would be about that little bundle of joy.

Many nights of unrest and paranoia followed. I posted constant watch on my sleeping prince, fearful that he would stop breathing in the middle of the night, or that something else would happen to him.

Alone to figure it all out was nothing more than trial and error most days. I did my best hoping and praying that it would be enough. Many days and nights I questioned my ability and worthiness to be a mother. Was I going to do him more harm than good? What exactly did I have to give to this little human being? The thought that this little person was totally dependent on me to mold him into everything that he could be terrified me. I wasn't all that I could be yet, so how on earth was I supposed to do that?

Cliff and I decided to give it another shot believing that every child deserved to have two parents in their lives. Sadly, this was also short-lived as he quickly proved that he was unwilling and incapable of committing to being a father.

Patricia's aunt had been amazing in allowing me to stay with her and her two children throughout my pregnancy and saw that I was in need of nothing. Now it was time to return but this time with a brand new baby. I knew that things would be great for the first few weeks as everyone marveled over the baby. But Aunty's house wasn't built for two families and she had her own life to live and her two young children to raise. Therefore, I also knew that it wouldn't be long before I would have to go out there and make a life for myself and Jermaine.

That time came in early November 1985 when I was nicely asked to make other living arrangements. The addition of an infant and a new mother took its toll on her family and her household. God bless her for opening her home and her heart to my son and I during our time of need.

My last attempt to seek assistance from Cliff was an epic failure and a few days later I gracefully packed up my child and a few necessities and moved into a hotel room after contacting Social Services for assistance.

That afternoon Jermaine and I hopped on the bus and in what seemed like hours later, we arrived in front of a fairly new looking building, the sign that hung near the roof read, Knight's Inn. I mustered up all the pride I could show on my face and entered the large foyer carrying Jermaine in my arms.

A snobby looking gentleman, who appeared to be no more than 5' 6" tall with greying hair, a pale complexion and light brown eyes stood behind the desk. "May I help you?" he asked, almost with pain in his voice as if he was about to do me a favour. "I would like a room for the night," I answered. He rudely consulted something on his desk and then placed a sheet of paper on the counter on which I had to write my name and contact information. After scribbling my signature, he snatched the sheet of paper off the desk and placed a room key on the counter to my left. The tag attached read '312'. "That will be $25.00," he said. I carefully shifted Jermaine to my left side and reached into my black leather purse and removed two $10.00 bills and one $5.00 bill from my tattered wallet and placed it in his hand. "Go to your left and up the elevator to the third floor, room #312," he said as he pointed with his left hand in the direction of the elevator. I quickly grabbed the key from his hand, afraid that if I stood there much longer, he would be able to read the terror, shame and loneliness on my face. I then made my way up the elevator and into room #312 without having to see anyone else with Jermaine in my left hand tightly snuggled against my chest.

The room was small and somewhat dark, the light switch on the wall to my right as I entered the room turned on a brass lamp with a white shade which was sitting on the small wooden desk situated in the left-hand corner of the room near the window. There was a large somewhat sturdy looking bed to my right covered with a multi-coloured bedspread almost like the one my mom had on the bed in the guest room at home.

I walked to the bed and pulled back the bed spread revealing crisp white sheets and three pillows covered in crisp white pillow cases. Well, at least it looks clean, I thought to myself. I then gently placed Jermaine on the bed. The little angel had slept peacefully throughout our entire afternoon ordeal.

The lamplight illuminating the room made it appeared a little more welcoming. The windows were covered with heavy looking drapes which hung from the ceiling to the floor. Several shades of green I think. I walked to the window and with both hands, pulled the drapes to each side. The afternoon sun burst in through the window like a thief in the night, forcing me to briefly close my eyes as they adjusted. The sunlight lit up the small room like a lantern in the night exposing a small wooden dresser with a medium size television perched on top in the middle of the room against the wall. Back towards the entrance door to the left was a small white door which led to a small washroom with a shower. It looked almost new, something I was happy to see, as I hate dirty bathrooms. A small closet stood across from the washroom on the right.

That night was the longest night of my life, as every little sound startled me. People laughing in the hallway, traffic outside on the street, you name it, it scared me. I watched as Jermaine slept peacefully on the bed and was tuned into his every move. The last thing I wanted was for him to fall off the bed and onto the dirty carpet. I couldn't sleep, I was afraid that someone would come into the room and steal my baby or that in my sleep, I would roll over and smother him. So I alternated between lying on the bed beside him making sure that he was breathing to staring aimlessly out the window at the traffic passing by.

Julie Barlow came into our lives the following day in November of 1985. I can only describe her as a social worker with a heart of gold. She may have stood 4' 7" tall with short brown hair and a medium build, but to me she was an angel sent from heaven to watch over me and my prince.

After witnessing our situation and hearing my full story, she immediately sprang into action. She told me that we would have to move to another less expensive hotel and that our cost would then be covered. She also explained that this was a short-term solution until she was able to arrange permanent housing for us. There was no solid time frame given but for the first time, I felt that there was actually someone on my side.

We checked out of the Knights Inn that afternoon along with Julie, and set off to the new location. It wasn't long before we arrived at our new temporary 'home'. This time, it was a long brown one-storey building that seemed to run on forever across the parking lot. The rooms had orange numbered doors all facing the parking lot and the sign at the front simply read 'Motel' I guess the rest of the name had burnt out. I gripped Jermaine even tighter to me knowing that this wasn't going to be anything like the hotel we were at last night, as Julie pulled away from us stating that she would check in with us tomorrow and that everything had been taken care of. The thought of having to stay there with my three-month-old baby for more than one night made me feel sick to my stomach but what other choice did I have.

I tried not to think about the length of time we may be stuck there as I entered the registration office. It was as though the tall white gentleman behind the desk was expecting us as he greeted us by name. "Elaine? And this must be little Jermaine," he said and then stated that he had already spoken with Julie. He then handed me a room key for room #106. "There's an ice machine there to your left and two vending machines with sandwiches and snacks in that walkway," he said as he pointed in the direction of our room. I kindly thanked him, took the key from his hand and scurried off towards room #106 wondering just how much Julie had told him about my situation.

Room #106, the big black numbers on the orange door read. There was a window to the right of the door covered with a heavy looking curtain that blocked my preview of what I was about to walk into. I reluctantly pushed the key into the lock and turned it to the left and pushed it forward revealing a dingy room with some heavy looking beige wallpaper on the walls. A queen size bed on the right sat low to the ground. A bedspread with a combination of orange, black and red pattern, which I thought showed no sense of style, at least not what I thought was style, covered a well-worn bed that dipped in the middle. Pulling back the bed spread with my right hand, I was surprised to see what appeared to be nice clean white sheets and three pillows covered with white pillow cases. I was still not sure how I was going to sleep on this thing never mind have my baby sleep on it. The rest of the room contained a small brown dresser, a colour television, a worn out looking grey coloured chair and a small wooden desk. A tiny, somewhat clean bathroom sat in the back of the room.

Later that evening, some baby supplies, clothing for me and a few other necessities were brought to the hotel by some friends. A short, uncomfortable visit followed as it was clear that no one knew what to say. Instead, they made small talk and played carefully with Jermaine. About an hour later they said their goodbyes and left the cramped little room as I spread my new comforter on top of the clean white sheets and laid Jermaine down to sleep. After watching him sleep for what seemed like hours, I finally laid down beside him and closed my eyes.

On December 15, 1985, I received a visit from Julie who took us to the most beautiful ground floor apartment in Meadowvale, I had ever seen. It wasn't very big, but it had two bedrooms, combination living/dining room, eat- in kitchen and a large bathroom. Most importantly, it was ours!

Several hours after our arrival, I watched through the side window as Julie drove away leaving us in our empty apartment furnished with only a small television, sitting on top of a milk crate and a crib for my prince which I strategically placed near the window in his bright blue room.

As I sat on the bare parquet floor in the living room, Jermaine in my arms, it hit me like a car hitting a brick wall. How on earth was

I going to raise this precious little human being and keep this roof over our head? Definitely not on Mother's Allowance.

All of a sudden that one missing high school credit didn't seem so insignificant. I needed to get my diploma and get a job so I could raise my son. At that moment, I knew that despite every one's disappointment and judgment we were going to be ok. I would make sure that he would want for nothing and he would always know that I love him, no matter what. He would accomplish much more than I ever could because I would give him every opportunity to become anything his heart desired. He was going to grow up healthy, strong and do great things.

So the hunt for employment began. I was already a statistic being 'a single black baby-mother' I wasn't about to raise my child on Mother's Allowance and Welfare as well. But what could I do without a High School Diploma other than retail which didn't pay very much, certainly not enough to raise a child on my own.

I had completed a business course a few years earlier and had some fairly good typing and organizational skills and considered myself reliable. So armed with that, pure determination and a touch of desperation, I completed a very flimsy resume and began to call every local business I could find in the phone book and ask if they were hiring. I combed through the Mississauga Times classified ads weekly. After months of relentless searching, I landed a job as a secretary at an industrial door company about twenty minutes from home. I was on top of the world.

After just over a year, I knew that there was more for me out there than this and began the hunt again. My new job offered more pay and flexibility for movement within the company, but again it just didn't feel right.

I had always had an interest in law and law enforcement and decided that it was time to return to school. Now twenty-three years old, I attended night school in order to get that last high school credit and then it was on to Sheridan College as part of their Continuing Education program which offered the perfect opportunity for me to begin my new journey to further my education and raise Jermaine at the same time. Courses in criminology and advocacy were my introduction to higher education and greater success. It was at that time, through my volunteer work with male inmates in custody, that I found my calling. Shortly before my twenty-fifth birthday, I began my career in the field of Corrections working with female offenders in custody and later transitioned to Youth Justice to work with youth in custody where I remain to this day. For the first time since giving birth, I was confident that I would be able to provide for myself and Jermaine on my own.

Jermaine and I spent every waking moment together when I wasn't at work or school, but working shifts started to take its toll. The money was great and gave me the means to give Jermaine everything his little heart desired and that I did. The best clothes, latest toys, you name it, he got it. Was that excessive? In hindsight, maybe, but that was my way of trying to compensate for my absence. Trips to the zoo, to various museums, Centre Island, Marine Land, Niagara Falls, Ontario Place, etc. followed. We were the perfect pair. Partners in crime some may say but was that enough?

Divine Intervention

When you set out to heal the body
ensure you also heal the mind.

On April 1, 1988, I awoke bright and early excited about the next few days of shopping and relaxation with my two older sisters. Something we had never done.

Everything had been arranged; kids were all taken care of. Things look promising for our well-deserved adventure.

The night before had been somewhat restless. I woke in the middle of the night after a dream in which myself and a few others were in a horrific car accident. I didn't remember much more about the dream other than driving in a vehicle, rolling down a cliff and hitting a large tree. The impact of the car hitting the tree jolted me out of my sleep.

Not being one who believed in dreams, I quickly shook it off and went on with packing the last few things for our trip. I threw a few more things in the bag and then to the kitchen to pack snacks for the road. I wasn't about to let anything get in the way of this highly anticipated getaway, especially not some stupid dream. With that, I said nothing of the dream to my sisters.

In the dream, I was driving in a thunderstorm. See nothing to worry about. No rain in the forecast for at least a week; the sun was shining and the day was beautiful. The perfect day to take my brand-new two-door Nissan Sentra on the open road for a test run. That was the first time I had the chance to take it on a long drive since I bought it only three weeks prior. It was spotless too. I had spent over an hour cleaning and waxing it the day before. She was fully loaded and ready for anything.

I hit the road to pick up Samantha and Sharon as soon as I loaded up the car. A few short minutes later, I arrived at Samantha's apartment building. She was obviously just as excited as I was because she was already standing in front of the building with two large bags by her side. She could never pack light. So after a game of Tetrus with her luggage in the trunk we managed to cram it all in. Next stop, Sharon. Good thing we all lived somewhat close to each other because I was already beginning to feel like a taxi driver. We pulled up to Sharon's several minutes later. A very pregnant Sharon came out the front door just as we pulled in. Nice, she only had one bag in her hand cause my poor car couldn't take anymore. She climbed into the front passenger seat and diligently buckled her seatbelt, with a little assistance I must add, then off we went.

Traffic was surprisingly light when we hit the road and my Nissan was driving like a dream. Music was bumping on the stereo and chatter about where we were going to shop first filled the air. Almost there, I thought, glancing at the Nappanee sign as we drove by on the 401. I reached over to find a new radio station because the one that had served us so well was quickly beginning to fade. Suddenly, out of nowhere, Pop! Pop! A feeling of gravel on my face and then nothing.

Why do the cars sound so loud? What happened to the music? Why can't I move? Oh my God, why can't I move?

The sound of the traffic got louder, the sound of voices I didn't recognize surrounded me. "Don't move! Don't move! Help is on its way," a voice repeated. I could feel my lips move, but couldn't hear the words coming out. The haze began to lift and I realized that I was lying on the gravel shoulder of Highway 401. There were several cars and a few transport trucks stopped on the highway blocking my view of the road and people running frantically all around.

"My sisters! My sisters!" I tried moving to find them, but was held down by the same woman who continued to tell me not to move. "I need to find my sisters!" Sirens screeched in the distance. "The ambulance is on its way, I just need you to stay still," she said,

"She pregnant." I heard someone in the distance yell. Sheer terror overcame me as I thought of Sharon and her unborn baby. "Is she ok? Is she ok!?" Oh my God, please don't let her lose the baby, please don't let her lose the baby. I could hear groaning coming from around my feet. That meant Sharon was close by. "Where's my other sister? Where's my other sister?"

"There's just the two of you" the lady replied. "No! Where's my other sister?"

"Go check the car!" she yelled.

I could hear the sound of shoes as they pounded on the gravel running away from where I laid helplessly on the ground. Several police cruisers and ambulances now lined the side of the highway and traffic seemed to have come to a slow crawl if not a complete stop as others got out of their vehicles to offer their assistance. Some just to see what was going on, I'm sure.

"There's someone in the car" I heard another voice shout. "She's fine." A sense of relief overcame me at that point and my concern switched back to Sharon. It may sound strange, but I don't remember feeling anything, although I'm sure I must have been in serious pain.

In all the confusion, I didn't even realize that I was being poked and prodded by this very tall gentleman in an official looking uniform. Paramedics had arrived on scene and were trying to determine the extent of my injuries. "I'm going to put this c-collar around your neck." I heard and next thing I know he was securing this hard plastic contraption around my neck. I remember how uncomfortable it felt as it stretched and pushed my chin in an unnatural position. I could feel myself being lifted up onto the stretcher as they prepared to put me in the ambulance. I could hear Samantha's voice in the background, I couldn't make out what she was saying, but at least I knew she was ok. Through the corner of my eye, I watched as they loaded Sharon into an ambulance which then took off down the highway sirens blazing, just before things went dark.

I opened my eyes to what felt like the warmth of the sun but quickly realized that it was actually the heat from a light shining above me as I laid on a bed in the emergency room. The room was white. Why's everything white? The light was bright in my eyes and prevented me from a clear view of what was happening around me. I heard a lot of chatter and shadow figures scurried all around. Machines with digital readouts and tubes were everywhere. A bag with clear liquid hung above my head with a tube leading down into my right arm. Sharon laid on a bed in an area right next to me, but all I could see was her protruding stomach. "Is she going to be okay? Is the baby okay?" I asked "The doctors will take good care of her." the nurse responded. With absolutely no concern for myself, all I could think was; How will I live with myself if she loses that baby? Nothing else mattered because I knew I could never live with the guilt. The curtains closed and again everything went black.

I must have fallen asleep or simply passed out from the medication because the next time I opened my eyes, my right leg was in a cast from toe to hip. A tall gentleman with dark brown hair and silver wire-rimmed glasses wearing a white lab coat entered the room.

"How are my sisters?" I immediately asked.

"Samantha will be fine, she's trying to reach your parents as we speak, he said. Sharon is being well taken care of in the room next-door. She has some minor injuries and is in some pain but will also be just fine."

I knew he was probably minimizing her injuries but I understood his motive. "The baby?" I asked.

"The baby is fine as well."

Tears began to fall down my face and the sense of relief was overwhelming. I think you could have told me that I had won the lottery and it wouldn't have felt as good as that news.

"You girls were all extremely lucky. From what I'm hearing, it was quite an accident." He continued.

Samantha then entered the room and asked the nurse who

stood by my bedside if she would speak with my dad. Apparently, he thought this was all an April fool's joke. Who could blame him? What were the odds that you would receive a phone call on April Fool's Day, informing you that more than half of your children were in the hospital after a serious car accident? The nurse then left the room along with Samantha.

Dr. Fredericks continued to explain that I had some muscle damage to my right leg and would need to wear the cast for six to eight weeks followed by extensive physiotherapy but that I would make a full recovery. "We'll still need to run a few more tests over the next few days and I've prescribed you some medication for the pain, but you'll be as good as new." He said as he scribbled something on my chart. "I will check in on you later," he said as he exited the room. Samantha came through the door followed by the nurse shortly after. "They're on their way. It'll take them a few hours to get here, but they're on their way." I took that as she was talking about our parents. I then drifted off to sleep.

The next morning, I woke to the sight of a police officer standing by my bedside. "Miss Murdock?"

"Yes."

"I am Officer Barrington. How are you feeling?"

Instinctively, I simply answered "okay," although I was far from okay. I was more curious as to why he was there. He pulled a small black notepad from his left hand shirt pocket followed by a pen.

"I was asked by my sergeant to investigate whether you had been drinking at the time of the accident and also to issue you a ticket for not wearing your seatbelt."

"I don't drink."

"Yes, your blood tests showed no alcohol in your system. Can you tell me what happened?"

"I don't remember much. I remember driving on the highway, changing the radio station and hearing a pop sound. The next thing I remember is feeling gravel on the side of my face, then opening my eyes to the sound of some woman's voice as I laid on the side of the highway."

"Where were you heading?"

"We were on our way to Montréal."

"Montréal!?"

"Yes, why? My sisters and I were on our way for a shopping weekend."

"Means you were driving eastbound?"

"Yes, why?"

"Your car was found on the westbound shoulder of the highway. At this point, it appears that the pop sound you heard was your tire blowing, two tires in fact. The car then rolled across the medium across the westbound lanes landing on the westbound shoulder. You and your sister Sharon were thrown clear of the vehicle as it rolled. Your sister Samantha states that she fell asleep in the back seat of the vehicle, as you and Sharon were talking, which is where she was found several meters from where you lay, virtually unharmed.

"Do you believe in God, Miss Murdock? Because from what I saw, there must have been some kind of divine intervention that saved you all from that car yesterday. As far as the ticket goes, I stopped by to see your vehicle before coming here. I'm sorry to say, but your car is a total write-off." That was really the least of my worries. "The front end of your car was so badly damaged that the steering wheel was pushed almost through the driver's seat. If you hadn't been thrown out of the vehicle we would not be having this conversation right now. I have never seen so much damage to the vehicle that did not result in a fatality. Given that, I can't with all good conscience give you a ticket for the seat belt violation. I'm glad you're all okay. Take care of yourself, Miss Murdock." He then briefly shook my hand and left the room.

Oh my God, I almost wiped out half my family! How does someone live with that? I laid there thinking that I must have been pulled out of the car for a reason. It was as if the Good Lord had said, "Oh no! I'm not ready for you yet. Your work is not yet done."

Several days later, Sharon and I were transferred from Nappanee Hospital via patient transport vehicle to two separate hospitals closer to home at the request of our parents. Samantha was able to return home. After several more days in the hospital, I was released while Sharon remained hospitalized to ensure that there was no risk to her pregnancy.

My road to recovery was slow, but I was determined to take full advantage of the new lease on life I had been given. I continued to visit my family doctor and endured months of physiotherapy to ensure my full physical recovery. However, I was totally oblivious to the emotional turmoil that traumatic event would later trigger.

Sharon was eventually released from the hospital and on August 26th, 1988 gave birth to my beautiful niece. Although she was born strong and healthy, I continually worried that she would show some kind of physical or mental defect as a result of the accident. Every chance I got, I watched my niece in secret for any signs that would give credibility to the guilt I felt. Thank God, those signs never came.

The Dark Times

Sometimes feeling sad is simply that,
the important thing is acknowledging
when it's much more.

Depression is defined as...

A state of extreme dejection or morbidly excessive melancholy; a mood of hopelessness and feelings of inadequacy often with physical symptoms such as loss of appetite, insomnia, etc.

Canadian Oxford Dictionary

In 2015, CAMH (Centre for Addiction and Mental Health Foundation reported that by 2020 depression will be the leading cause of disability around the world.

Psychology Today wrote: "A depressive disorder is not the same as a passing blue mood. It is not a sign of personal weakness or a condition that can be willed or wished away. People with a depressive illness cannot merely "pull themselves together" and get better. Without treatment, symptoms can last for weeks, months or years."

By Jermaine's sixth birthday, the constant struggle to balance life, my guilt from the accident, self-care and the never ending demands of single parenthood began to manifest into increased sick days at work, sleeping all day, staying up all night, lack of appetite and frequent mood swings.

Yes, you guessed it, I was beginning to suffer from depression. The problem was that I didn't know that I was clinically depressed. All I knew was that I was convinced that I could never be the mother Jermaine deserved. This constant feeling of inadequacy led me from days of feeling on top of the world like super mom, to wondering what my purpose here was and why God thought that I could raise this child. Never mind trusting me to raise him on my own.

I went from playing and laughing with Jermaine one minute to excusing myself and melting into a puddle of tears on the kitchen, bathroom or living room floor, where ever it hit me. I diligently tried to put on a solid and positive face in front of Jermaine and all those who slowly began to re-enter my life. Jermaine was always clean, fed, well-dressed and appeared well adjusted and happy. He was polite, caring, friendly and smart.

Me? I now had a great full-time job that paid well and I enjoyed which meant no more Mother's Allowance or subsidized rent. To all those looking in, things were looking up. It seemed as though I might actually have this mother thing figured out and adulthood was beginning to settle on me as well, but inside I was in constant turmoil.

As I continued to spin into the depths of hell, I could barely get through a day without multiple meltdowns. I couldn't wait for Jermaine to go off to school so I could exercise my only sense of relief: a good, long, sometimes, never-ending cry on the floor of my choice.

The day I could no longer hold back the tears and found myself crying in front of Jermaine over a bowl of cereal, was the day I decided to go see my family doctor. He was the only person I could think of that wouldn't judge me (because of his professional responsibilities) and even if he did, it wouldn't be to my face. He had been my doctor for a few years now and had a very open and trusting approach to patient care.

As soon as Jermaine was safely at school, I returned to the apartment, picked up the phone and dialed the number. Jan, Dr. Brown's secretary's cheery voice answered the phone on the third ring.

"Dr. Brown's office, please hold," she said and before I could agree to hold, the line went silent. That was all I needed to collapse onto the kitchen floor in full blown hysteria. By the time Jan came back on the phone, "How can I help you?" she said. I could barely get a breath in, never mind words out of my mouth. I managed to spit out my name and told Jan that I needed to see Dr. Brown as soon as possible. "What's going on Elaine?" she asked. I started to explain what had been happening and that I didn't know what else to do and had no one else to call. She kindly asked me if I thought that I could make the ten-minute drive to the office and said that she would squeeze me into the schedule upon my arrival.

The ten-minute drive seemed like an hour, as I tried to fight off the feelings of despair and wipe the tears from my eyes so that I could focus on the road. I pull into the parking lot in front of the tall eight storey light beige building. I actually got a parking space close to the entrance as it was still pretty early, I suppose.

The building contained primarily health care based businesses that were just about to open. It would be a zoo in an hour or so once all the patients arrived for their various appointments, tests and other treatments.

I walked through the corridor to the elevator, keeping my bloodshot eyes focused on the floor to conceal them from anyone I may run into on the way, and pushed the shiny silver 'up' button on the wall to the right of two big silver doors. The sound of a short bell announced the arrival of the elevator. Both doors opened, revealing an empty shell with mirrors all around the top half and some wooden looking finishes across the bottom half. The brass coloured support bar that ran through the middle and around the inside looked freshly polished not yet marred by greasy fingerprints. As I entered the elevator, I immediately pushed the white plastic button labeled '3' hoping that no one else would get in with me. I really didn't want to be seen in that state. The elevator soon began to move towards the third floor, with a squeal. Three bells announced my arrival on the third floor and I quickly exit the elevator wiping the tears from my cheek so as not to look like a total nut job when I walked into Dr. Brown's office.

I slowly made my way down the narrow hallway to the left of the elevator trying to regain my composure and figure out what I was going to say. I arrived at unit 310 and slowly turned the doorknob clockwise and pushed the door open. I was quite surprised to see four other patients already in the waiting room directly in front of me. Jan greeted me with her regular cheery voice and asked for my Health Card. I immediately handed her the card as I had already anticipated that she would ask for it and had it in my hand. After verifying the information on the card she handed it back to me and informed me that Dr. Brown had not yet arrived in the office but should be here shortly as he was just finishing his early morning rounds at the hospital. She then stated that she would squeeze me in first as the rest of the day was booked solid. I fought back the tears of disappointment and thanked her before going to sit with the four other patients on one of the molded orange plastic chairs in the small waiting area. I sat quietly on the chair trying not to make eye contact with the older woman sitting across from me, worried that I would just break down again. She glanced up at me as I sat and flashed me a polite smile as if to say hello without words. Her smile revealed several wrinkles around her red lipstick coloured mouth and crow's feet around her eyes. Her teeth were a light shade of yellow which made her appear older than she probably was. I picked up an outdated magazine from the small table next to my chair and began to flip through the pages in an attempt to temporarily occupy my mind as I waited.

Several minutes later, the office door swung open and in walked Dr. Brown. He quickly greeted us in passing and scurried to his office in the back after also greeting Jan, who sat behind the large receptionist counter.

It wasn't long before I heard my name called. I quickly approached the desk, "He's ready for you. Room two." Jan said. I walked down the hallway followed by Jan holding my patient chart against her chest with her left hand. Once in room two, she asked me a few short questions, jotted down the answers on my chart and then exited the room stating that Dr. Brown would be right in.

There sure are a lot of posters on the walls, I thought: coloured charts about asthma with very detailed illustrations, informational posters about high blood pressure, a well-illustrated chart depicting the various stages of the embryo during pregnancy and different posters about new medications and their usage. Then there was the blood pressure instrument with cuff, the thermometer and a few other shiny looking things I couldn't identify.

Dr. Brown entered the room wearing brown dress pants, a beige button-down collared shirt and brown loafers. He was always a smart dresser, I remember thinking. He sat down on the rolling chair by the small desk and glanced at my patient chart. "So, Elaine, what's been going on?" he asked. Tears immediately started to well up in my eyes and slowly roll down my face. He reached over and removed the small Kleenex box from the desk and handed to me. Not knowing where to start, I simply shouted "I don't know if I can do this anymore!" After that, my soul came pouring out as if I had no shut-off switch. I told him about the uncontrollable crying, lack of appetite, mood swings, not being able to go to work, and about the unexpected challenges and isolation I had been feeling since becoming a single mother. That I had begun to question my ability to be a mother and feared that I was doing Jermaine more harm than good with my constant emotional breakdowns. No mother wants to have her child witness her occasional moments of weakness. With me, it was a constant occurrence and I could no longer hide or shake off those episodes.

It actually felt good to get it all out. Dr. Brown, although only a family doctor, sat quietly and listened, showing concern and great empathy as I spoke. When I finally stopped talking Dr. Brown asked

"Where is Jermaine?" I told him that he was at school and wasn't due home until this afternoon.

"Do you have someone who can help you with Jermaine?" he asked. "No. We'll be ok."

"I think it's a good idea if you get someone to come help you with Jermaine for a little while. Things will get better. It's not unusual for new mothers to feel overwhelmed. I'm going to give you something to help with the mood swings and then refer you to see Dr. Patrick over at Credit Valley Hospital. It may take a little while before he has an opening, but someone from his office will contact you once they receive the referral. In the meantime, make sure to take these as directed and come and see me immediately should things get worse." He then handed me a prescription from his prescription pad and asked me to book a follow-up appointment with Jan for next week on my way out.

I thanked him for his time and watched as he left the room pulling the door in behind him leaving me to gather myself together. I splashed some cold water on my face from the small sink in the room and used that rough brown paper towel to dry it off hoping that it would help reduce the redness of my eyes and then exited the room. I approached Jan's desk and again was greeted by her warm smile. I told her that I needed to book a follow-up appointment with Dr. Brown for next week. She began to search through the calendar on her computer and with hesitation in her voice informed me that Dr. Brown was all booked for next week and that there was nothing available for another three weeks. I guess she must have seen the desperation in my face because she immediately said that she would give me a call first thing next week and see if she can squeeze me in. I thanked her for her efforts and headed toward the waiting room.

Re-entering the waiting room, I could see the resentment on the older woman's face as she stared at me. I didn't blame her, after all, I did arrive after her and it had been more than a half-hour since I went in to see Dr. Brown. I managed to muster up a faint smile for her and quickly exited the office.

Rushing home, I tried to think of who I could get to help me out with Jermaine until this passed. Sadly, no one came to mind. I got home just in time to get Jermaine from school and fell right back into the mommy mode.

The next few months were a roller coaster of emotions and medication to keep going. One day just prior to Jermaine's seventh birthday, I reluctantly called Jermaine's father as I remembered he had said that his parents (now that they had finally come around to accept Jermaine) had offered to help with Jermaine if needed. As much as every fibre of my being wanted to keep Jermaine as far away from those people as possible, I had to put Jermaine's wellbeing first and I knew that I was in no shape to adequately take care of him like this. Later that day, I packed Jermaine into the red Dodge Shadow and drove to his grandparents' home in an upscale neighborhood in Mississauga where Cliff also lived.

We pulled into driveway and again that little voice in the back of my head told me to just turn the car around with my child and figure it out on my own. Once again I ignored it and got Jermaine out of the car and headed to the front door. I rang the doorbell and secretly hoped that no one would answer. One. Two. Three. No answer, good.

Just as I was about to turn around and head for the car, the door opened and in we went. As Jermaine played in the family room, I sat with his grandparents and told them what had been going on and then asked if they would be willing to take care of Jermaine for a short period of time until I got myself back on-track. They showed great concern for Jermaine quickly offering to give him the one thing I was convinced that I could not give him. Stability.

In my broken state, I agreed, believing that it would only be a few weeks or worst case scenario a few months. Even though a part of me was saying don't do it. The larger part was telling me that it was the best decision for Jermaine right then and that I had no other option if I wanted to avoid CAS (Children's Aid Society) involvement. I should have felt relieved, now that there was someone to help, someone who wanted the best for Jermaine just as much as I did. Instead I felt even more like a failure, unsure of my decision and there was still something in my gut that just didn't feel right. I had to remind myself that this was for Jermaine and not me and that it was temporary as we left the house that evening.

Now that I look back, I feel that unbeknown to me, his grandparents took advantage of my emotional state in order to seize their opportunity to take my child from me and that it really wasn't about helping me at all.

That night the drive home was slow and long as I desperately held back the tears and tried to explain to Jermaine that he was going to stay with grandma and grandpa for a little while. I tried to break it down as simply as possible in hopes that his little mind would understand. "You know how mommy is always crying for no reason?" I said "That's because mommy isn't feeling well and needs some time so that she can get better," I explained. He looked at me with his big brown eyes as I pulled him close and told him that I loved him very much and that he would not have to stay with his grandparents for very long.

The next day, we spent the afternoon packing his things for what I convinced myself was going to be a great adventure for him. With a very heavy heart, I dropped him off at his grandparents' home that evening.

Jermaine seemed to be settling in well at the grandparents when out of the blue, I received a phone call from them requesting to speak with me. Upon arriving at the house, I was ushered into the family room once again. This time, I was met by Jermaine's sweet little face. Oh my gosh, he's changed so much and it hasn't even been that long. Jermaine sat playing with his toys next to me as his grandparents explained that they were presented with an opportunity and would love to register Jermaine into a private school in Jamaica because they realized that he was an extremely bright little boy and that the school system there was much better than the one here as it was based on the British education system. They went on to convincingly state that they wanted to make sure that he had the best opportunities in life and they believed that this opportunity would give him a great head start. That was all I ever wanted for Jermaine and the thought of them being willing and able to offer him that was a blessing. With that, I agreed to their offer and within the next few days provided them with a signed letter giving them temporary responsibility for Jermaine and permission to take Jermaine out of the country. That document would come back to seriously bite me in the butt later on in this journey.

Determined to make things better for Jermaine's return, I started to get things back on track, I forced myself to return to work and took much comfort in the belief that Jermaine was in this amazing school program being cared for in ways I was unable to at that time. Things were looking up, or so I thought.

This effort was short lived as my valiant efforts proved to be too much and my emotions began to once again spin out of control. First, the feelings of profound sadness, worthlessness and desperation. Then the mood swings returned with a vengeance, I stopped eating, I began to sleep all day and couldn't get it together enough to continue to go to work. All attempts to come to terms with my decision miserably failed.

I began to question my existence, my purpose and my worth. After all, I had failed at being the one thing that most women long for. The one thing that the good Lord saw fit to bless me with and I had no idea how I was going to fix it. Was I really capable of being a mother? Could God have made a mistake in thinking that I should be blessed with this amazing responsibility? Or was this His way of telling me that He had changed His mind? Then thoughts of suicide began to creep into my mind. Although I knew that I could and would never take my own life, I knew that I had to do something to help myself get through this and fast. I really had no idea what was going on. All I knew was that I was tired and felt like I had nothing left.

My first trip to Credit Valley Hospital was the result of a desperate 911 call made by my sister Sharon when she became extremely concerned for my well-being after several attempts to reach me by phone had failed.

You guessed it, I had fallen into a deep depression and had suffered what they called a nervous breakdown.

That night I met Dr. Patrick, he was attentive and caring. He questioned me about the conditions, which led to my admission and after what felt like the Spanish Inquisition, told me that he would like me to check into the inpatient unit at the hospital for treatment. He informed me that I could go home that evening to get my things in order, pack a few things and then report to the hospital the next morning.

Oh my God, this was going to be embarrassing, what was I going to tell my family, friends, my employer? Oh, by the way, I have to check myself into the 'loonie bin', see you all soon.

How was I going to live this down, how was I ever going to prove to everyone that I wasn't 'crazy' I thought as I left the hospital and headed home. Mental health was generally misunderstood back then, even by me, which only fueled the anxiety I was feeling not to mention the stigma I would have to deal with once this was all over.

Another sleepless night was followed by a morning that arrived a lot faster than I had hoped. I pulled myself up out of bed, threw on a navy blue Adidas tracksuit a pair of well-worn Puma running shoes and got my sister up off the sofa where she had spent the night. I went into the bathroom, brushed my teeth, washed my face and looked at myself in the mirror to a reflection that I did not recognize. I didn't even bother to comb my hair as it really wouldn't have made much difference at that point.

Arriving at the hospital we approached the information counter where we were greeted by a young man who couldn't have been any more than eighteen years old. Obviously a volunteer. He was pleasant enough and immediately asked how he could be of assistance. His big green eyes slimmed to a near close when he smiled. He had dark brown hair which looked like he had just come from the barber. His crisp white shirt showed that he took pride in his self and his work. "We're looking for the In-Patient Psychiatric Unit," Sharon said, as I was too embarrassed to speak. "Down this hallway to the end, then turn right, go to the end and you'll see a reception desk just before a set of double doors. You'll have to check in there," he said as he pointed us in the right direction. Sharon thanked him for his assistance and we proceeded down the hallway. The hospital was busy. People heading in every direction. Some in more of a hurry than others. Nurses scurrying from one area to another, people purchasing flowers and gifts for their loved ones in the gift shop and others buying coffee after a long night, I assumed.

A few moments later we arrived at the reception desk just outside a set of brown double doors. The sign read; Psychiatric Unit. Another pleasant looking gentleman sat behind the counter. He was probably in his early thirties and wore a light brown wool sweater and black pants. His light brown hair looked like he was due for a cut and his teeth required some immediate attention. He greeted us with a faint smile as if embarrassed about his teeth. "How can I help you?" he asked. Sharon told him my name and informed him that I was asked to report there by Dr. Patrick after seeing him in Emergency last night. He glanced down at the computer on the desk in front of him and punched a few keys. "Ah yes, Miss Murdock" he stated. "May I have your Health Card?" he asked. I reached into my pocket and retrieved the card and handed it to him. After confirming the information on my card, he handed it back to me and I quickly returned it to my pocket. Sharon and I stood there while he punched a few more keys on the computer and then picked up the phone receiver beside him. Almost immediately the double doors opened and a slim lady dressed in a light pink nurses uniform and bright white running shoes exited. "Elaine?" she said as she stretched out her left hand to greet me. That threw me off a little because I am so used to people extending their right hand. "I'm Michelle." I shook her hand and then introduced Sharon who was standing beside me. "I understand that you'll be staying with us for a little while," she casually said as she walked back towards the double doors. "I guess," I responded as Sharon and I followed her through the doors which lead into the Unit. It was cold, not very inviting at all and I wondered how many others were being kept there.

Michelle seemed very nice and tried to show that she understood how I was feeling. She even tried to reassure me that I was not the first mother to feel overwhelmed. She stood about 5' tall with light brown shoulder length hair and a small build. She seemed a little young to be a nurse but none the less she appeared to have the compassion I always thought a nurse should have especially in that kind of environment. She walked us down a small hallway and into a small room that contained only a bed and a small table. I placed my bag on the table and sat on the bed looking around the room, which was pretty depressing in its self: bare walls and a small window with not much of a view. That's ok because I really had no intention of getting comfortable. Sharon just watched with a look of concern on her face. I tried not to cry as I knew that would only make things worse.

"This will be your room," Michelle said. "I'll give you a few minutes to gather your thoughts and say goodbye to your sister, then I will be back to go over a few things and take you on a short tour later this afternoon," she said as she left the room. I sat on the bed mortifyingly embarrassed at the thought that I was in a place like that. All I wanted to do was sleep and to be left alone. What the hell did I need a tour for? I wasn't planning on leaving that room unless it was to go home. Sharon sat with me for a while and then left as I sat on the bed trying to figure out what went wrong.

Michelle reappeared at my door about fifteen minutes later with a few sheets of paper in her hands. After reviewing the information on the forms I was asked to sign in various places. She then gathered the signed forms and exited the room.

Late that afternoon, she returned. "Are you ready?" she asked. "Not really," I responded. I reluctantly got up off the bed and followed Michelle out the door with her insistence. Boy, for a little thing she just doesn't give up. We walked through the unit, down hallways passing a few other patients milling around. Most of them looked very sad and some a little disoriented. Their meds I guessed. The place was actually pretty clean and didn't look much different from other parts of the hospital that I had been in for various reasons over the years. It wasn't like the 'psychiatric hospitals' depicted on television, where people were all walking around like zombies bouncing off walls, pulling their hair out and screaming. Or so drugged up that they just sat on chairs in a corner slobbering all over themselves. I didn't see any padded cells or people in straight-jackets either.

Michelle introduced me to a few of the other nurses on duty

and a few of the other patients who we came across. I was shown where I would be expected to participate in group activities, and a small room where I could watch television with the other patients. There was also a small kitchen area where I could get a snack or store goodies that family brought in during visits. Michelle explained the daily schedule and visiting hours and guidelines. The more she spoke the more frightened I got. Thoughts of being kept here against my will began to flood my mind and push my anxiety levels through the roof.

I knew that I had hit rock bottom when I finally realized that it was a locked unit. That meant that I could not leave without my doctor' s permission. What???!!!! How on earth did I let things get that bad? Me, Elaine Murdock, the rock of Gibraltar. Sad to say but I was happy to see my room again after the tour as it meant that I could lay down, shut everybody out and go to sleep and that's exactly what I did.

I don't remember much after laying on that not-so-comfortable bed but someone must have come into the room as I slept. I open my eyes to see a small tray on the desk beside me with a small bowl, one of those mini boxes of Corn Flakes, a carton of milk, a fruit cup and some limp looking toasted brown bread when I awoke. "Breakfast?? Wow!" I actually slept through the night.

Later that morning, a heavy-set nurse rushed into my room to inform me that I was expected to attend a morning art class. Art? Do I look like I want to paint any damn picture? I explained to her that I was exhausted and just wanted to sleep. She annoyingly explained that participation in programs was an expectation and important part of my treatment plan as instructed by Dr. Patrick. She then agreed to let me rest as I had my first appointment with Dr. Patrick that afternoon. With that, I laid back down and drifted off to sleep.

Shortly after lunch, Michelle appeared at my room door and escorted me down a brightly lit hallway and into a small office where I was greeted by Dr. Patrick. I recognized the name on the office door just before she pushed it open. I didn't really pay much attention to his looks when we first met in the emergency. I guess you could say that I had more important things on my mind.

He was a tall, heavy set white gentleman with long dark hair slightly greying, which was pulled back in a ponytail. He doesn't look anything like a psychiatrist well, at least not what I thought one would look like. He didn't have a long couch, where I was supposed to lay while I poured out my heart and soul to him, in his office either. He wore grey dress pants and a light blue dress shirt. He was one of those people whose age was hard to guess so I'll leave that part alone.

He sat quietly behind his large wooden desk and introduced himself, motioning for me to have a seat in the small leather chair in front of the desk. I eased into the chair as tears began to slowly run down my face, this time from fear. How was I going to talk to this man? We have nothing in common; he wasn't even female so how could he possibly understand the challenges and effects of motherhood, never mind single-motherhood? How on earth was he going to help me and most importantly, how long would I have to stay here?

Sitting in the chair I began to think of things he would want me to say in order to let me go home. What if he decided that I was 'crazy' and decided that my stay here needed to be a lengthy one? Who was going to look after Jermaine when he returned home? Our first session was what I would call unproductive. Not much was said as I didn't know where to start and I was afraid of saying the wrong thing. Dr. Patrick asked a few questions to which I gave very vague answers, if any. This is a waste of time, I remember thinking. By day three, I finally realized that I was going to have to buy into the process if I had any hope of getting out of there and back to Jermaine. Once I began to open up and really give it a chance, I realized how easy he was to talk to and the words just began to flow as if someone had turned on a tap.

For the next three weeks, I met with Dr. Patrick daily and spoke about my childhood, my first few years with Jermaine, the accident, my niece, my job and my decision to send Jermaine to Jamaica. He made me feel comfortable making it much easier to speak although I wasn't sure how talking about all this stuff was going to help me. Maybe it was the medication. The rest of my time was spent talking with some of the other patients and watching television, some small activities but mostly sleeping as I tried to regain control of myself.

The morning of my release, unlike every other morning since my admission, took what seemed like forever to come as I could barely sleep despite the medication I was given. Michelle was there to see me off, reminding me that I would now be an out-patient and was expected to see Dr. Patrick twice a week and to continue to take my medication as prescribed. She made sure that she reminded me of the importance of taking the medication only as directed as it was extremely addictive and dangerous if misused. She then handed me a prescription and a schedule of my next few appointments.

The drive home was slow and silent, my mind going a million miles a minute thinking of all the things I was going back to. Was everything going to be different now that I had spent three weeks locked away from reality? I sure hoped so because I knew that it wouldn't be long before Jermaine would be home and I needed to be ready to be the mother he needed. I thought of what I would say the first time I saw him and again began to question my decision to send him to his grandparents. Did I do the best thing for him or would my decision change his life map forever? The one thing I did know was that my experience in the hospital had given me a new perspective. I began to feel that I was indeed capable of raising my son and that I didn't have to be perfect. All I had to do was to love him and do the best I could.

You know when people say not to ignore the feeling in the pit of your stomach or the hair on the back of your neck standing up? Well, this is one time when I truly wished that I had acknowledged my stomach because things were about to get real ugly!

When Jermaine first left for Jamaica, I received regular reports from his grandparents as to how well he was adjusting to his new school and life in Jamaica. This helped to ease the anxiety and doubt I had over my decision to allow them to send him away. Although I wasn't allowed to speak with him directly because his grandparents thought that would only interfere with his adjustment, these updates gave me something to look forward to. Then the updates began to fade, phone calls went unanswered and unreturned. There went those hairs on the back of my neck again.

As Christmas break drew near, I anxiously prepared myself for my prince's return, but something just didn't feel right. I began to place frantic calls to his grandparents and Cliff to no avail trying to find out the exact date of his return. Then finally, late one evening Mrs. Charles answered the phone. The pleasantries she usually tried to portray in her voice when we spoke was clearly absent which made her tone almost hostile.

She informed me that Jermaine would not be returning home for Christmas and that he would return in the summer at the end of the school year as he was doing so well and they did not want to interrupt his progress.

I was blown away and crippled with disbelief. I couldn't believe what I was hearing. I insisted that they bring him home for the holidays and she refused. That call ended and I hung up the phone in shock. What the heck was going on? Why won't they bring back my child? God, I hope nothing happened to him. I began to form all kinds of crazy scenarios in my head like: he's been kidnapped and they just don't want to tell me.

I quickly shook those thoughts out of my head as I knew that if I continued on that path I would only find myself back in the 'loonie bin'. I forced myself to come to terms with the fact that there wasn't anything I could do as I didn't even have an address or even a name of the person he was staying with in Jamaica to try to contact him directly. Yes, I was desperate and trusting when the agreement was made and them being his grandparents, I felt no need to get that kind of information at the time.

So with no other choice, I began to plan for his summer return and upcoming birthday. With no Jermaine in my near future, I began to focus on getting myself back on track with work and even started going to the gym again in an effort to keep myself busy. I found a beautiful apartment in Brampton just five minutes away from work and thought that it would be a great opportunity for Jermaine and I to start fresh when he returned but even more importantly, to put some distance between his grandparents and us.

The building was brand new and we would be amongst the first few people to move in. There was a nice little park right downstairs and the apartment had a great view from the eighth floor. Jermaine will love this, I thought. He'd never lived in a high-rise apartment before. The day I received the keys gave me an amazing sense of accomplishment I hadn't felt in a long time. This was the first time I had actually found a home by myself. I did the searching, contacted the landlord, signed the lease all by myself. Not like our place in Mississauga, that was all my worker Julie's doing. All I had to do that time was just sign where she told me and move right in.

Preparing for the move and getting Jermaine's new room ready became my focus for the next few months. I had also found a new passion for my work with youth through my new understanding of mental illness, particularly depression and applied it daily. Things were looking up. So never in my wildest dreams did I envision what came next.

June of 1993, I was ecstatic when Cliff told me that Jermaine was back home. I attributed the fact that his grandparents didn't bring him directly home to me to the fact that I had moved and chose not to share my new address with them.

Needless to say, I couldn't wait to see him and bring him home. I immediately picked up the phone and anxiously dialed the number. One ring, two rings, three rings, no answer. That's weird. I hung up the phone double checked the number I had dialed and carefully dialed again making sure not to misdial. The phone began to ring again and my heart started to pound in my chest. What if he answers? What was I going to say? Again the phone rang without answer. "Ok, let's try Cliff." I reached for my brown leather bound phone book, opened it and flipped to the C section and looked for Cliff's number just to make sure I was dialing the right number as it had been some time since I called him. That call also went unanswered.

Not knowing what else to do, I called my sister Samantha and told her what was going on and asked her to come with me to go get Jermaine. She quickly agreed. As I waited for her arrival, I tried to think of how I was going to handle this situation should it go south. I tried to convince myself that everything was going to be ok and that Jermaine would be home sleeping in his own bed that evening. Nothing could have been further from the truth.

Samantha arrived a short time after and I quickly jumped into her car and we took off for Mississauga. We pulled into the driveway about twenty minutes later. As soon as I got out of the car, my eyes were automatically drawn upwards to the second floor of the house. There in the window of one of the front bedrooms was Jermaine with a big smile on his face, looking out the window as if he was expecting me. My heart sank, I hadn't seen my baby in almost a year and I wondered how much he had changed. All I knew was that I couldn't wait to hold him in my arms and tell him how much I missed him and to apologize for leaving him for so long.

I ran up the driveway, leaving Samantha in the car and rang the doorbell. I patiently waited for an answer, but there was none. Again, I rang the doorbell this time followed by a knock on the door a well just in case the doorbell was broken. Still no answer. I found it strange that Jermaine didn't come to the door but didn't put much more thought than that into it. I knew someone else was home because they would not have left Jermaine alone in the house.

A few moments later the door finally opened and in the doorway stood Mrs. Charles who quickly informed me that Jermaine was not leaving that house and refused to return my child to me. She wouldn't even let me see him. She then closed the door leaving me standing on the doorstep totally flabbergasted.

I walked back out to the driveway where Samantha was now standing watching Jermaine in the window. It tore at my soul as I watched Jermaine standing crying and calling out to me from the upstairs window.

I stood helplessly in the driveway as my baby appeared to be being held against his will. Total anger quickly replaced my feelings of helplessness and determined to get my baby out of that house, I called the police, convinced that they would come and remove Jermaine from the house and return him to me. After all, I was his mother.

We anxiously awaited the arrival of the police, who were going to save the day, for what seemed like forever. Then finally a police cruiser turned the corner followed by another. I was now certain that things were going to work out as they slowly approached the house. An older gentleman exited the first cruiser followed by a very young looking female, must be a rookie, I thought but didn't really care at that point as long as they got Jermaine out of that house. I frantically tried to hold myself together as I informed the officers that my son was being held by his grandparents who were refusing to return him to me. I then pointed to the bedroom window where Jermaine stood weeping. I went on to explain that they have a written agreement which gave them temporary guardianship of Jermaine when I was going through some rough times last year and asked for their help. I further explained that this was not a court document and no legal counsel was involved with the agreement and that I had only written it so that they could send Jermaine to Jamaica for school.

The older officer wrote diligently in his little black notebook as I spoke and then asked my name, address and phone number which he also recorded in his notebook. He then informed me that they would go speak with the grandparents and then walked up to the front door leaving Samantha and I in the driveway.

Several agonizing minutes passed before I saw the officers emerge from the house. I was beyond shocked to see that Jermaine was not by their side. Instead they proceeded to explain that the signed agreement that I had given Jermaine's grandparents did not contain an end date and that I essentially had given them custody of him by drafting and signing that agreement. Tears of sheer terror and panic began to run down my face as his words began to blur into incoherent sounds exiting his mouth. I braced myself against the car as my legs began to give way to the weight of my grief. Finally, he explained that there was nothing that they could do and that this matter would have to be sorted out in court. This is not a 'matter' this is my baby we're talking about. I stood totally broken in the driveway as the two cruisers pulled away from the house and disappeared around the corner. I could still see Jermaine in the window, now in what looked like full blown hysteria. I stood wailing in the driveway incapable of any rational thought as Samantha tried to console me to no avail.

As we embarked on the never-ending drive home, I tried to understand what had just happened. Did they truly believe that I had just given them my child? A child that I had carried for nine months and raised on my own, with no help from anyone including them, for the first seven years of his life. Nah!! I convinced myself that they were just upset that their time with Jermaine had come to an end and that once they had the night to think about what had just happened and realized that I did want my child back they would come to terms with my decision and return him to me.

That night seemed never-ending as I tried to fathom life without my prince. That truly was not an option. I decided then to seek the assistance of a lawyer to ensure that didn't happen. The gloves were on and if it was a fight the Charles's wanted I was primed to give it to them. I was about to go to war with the Titans!

My Battle for Custody

*There's no limit to what a mother is
capable of when backed into a corner.*

The next morning, I reluctantly climbed out of bed knowing that I had to be at work for 6:30am. and would probably have to search for a family lawyer, should I not hear from Jermaine's grandparents.

I had to pull myself together as I had just begun to settle back into the high demands of my job and knew that I could not afford to miss any more time at work. I put on my uniform and ran out the door at the last minute to ensure my timely arrival.

It was early afternoon when I heard a page over the PA system "CO Murdock please report to the front vestibule", I immediately left my assigned area and walked to the vestibule where I was greeted by a member of the Sheriff's department who, after verifying my name, proceed to hand me a large brown envelope and quickly exited the vestibule.

I re-entered the building and hesitantly opened the large brown envelope and removed the papers inside. I began to read through the document and quickly realized that It was a subpoena for me to appear in court as Jermaine's grandparents were seeking full custody of him claiming that I suffered from mental illness and was therefore unfit and incapable of raising him. They were using my battle with depression and subsequent hospitalization against me. The document went on to state that they had the financial means to raise him, inferring that I did not. I almost fell to my knees as they weakened beneath me, but had to be mindful that I was being watched by another officer who was bursting with curiosity, I'm sure. I was in total shock that these people whom I trusted and thought were trying to help me were actually trying to take my son from me. Who did they think they were? I know money is helpful when raising a child but it doesn't make you a parent. Plus, they already had a son, why did they want mine?

What now? How was I going to fight these people for my child? I was a single mother who had mood swings and no money in comparison to their financial resources. I didn't have the slightest clue as to how or where to find a lawyer or even how the court system worked in that situation.

Could they actually take my child? After all, I had given them temporary guardianship via a signed agreement. All I knew was that I had to try and like a mama bear protecting her cub I prepared to go to war for my child. No way were they going to get away with this. Money or no money I was committed to fighting them with everything I had. The new found strength and confidence I found while in the hospital was about to be put to the ultimate test.

Trying to hide my tears, I went to the Shift Office called my manager and told her what had just happened and that I needed to leave immediately. I barely waited for her response before putting down the receiver and with the envelope tightly gripped in my hand bolted down the hall through the three secure doors and out into the parking lot. I was so blind with rage that it took me a few seconds to locate my car that sat directly in front of me.

I peeled out of the parking lot and headed to the Meadowvale Town Centre near our old house as I had remembered a lawyer's office located near the entrance. Pulling into the parking lot, I quickly retrieved the envelope from the seat beside me, jumped out of my vehicle and ran towards the mall entrance clutching the brown envelope against my chest as my purse dangled off my left shoulder.

The sign above the entrance read: Lawyers Office. There was a polite looking woman sitting behind the desk as I entered.

"May I help you?"

"I need to see a lawyer,"

"What kind of lawyer?"

Not knowing how to answer the question I simply handed her the large brown envelope. She took the envelope from me, opened it, removed the papers inside and as I stood watching, began to read the document. "Ms. Murdock, please have a seat, someone will be with you shortly," she said as she got up from behind her desk and entered the back area. I watched as she disappeared down a short hallway. She wore the most amazing pair of yellow pumps with silver buckles. Yes, I noticed because I have a thing for shoes.

A few minutes later, a sharply dressed woman wearing a tailored navy blue pants suit, white blouse and bright red patent leather pumps emerged. She stood about 5' 7" in her heels, dark brown hair cut in a bob style, light brown complexion (almost beige if I had to be precise) and a reassuring smile. "Ms. Murdock?" she asked as she extended her right hand to greet me. "I'm JoAnne Winters, please come this way." I followed her down the short hallway and approached what looked like a small boardroom. "This way," she said as she motioned with her right hand for me to enter the room. She quickly followed and closed the door behind her. The room was small with light blue walls and a large wooden table with six leather chairs sat in the centre. A copy of a Norman Rockwell print completed the look. Nothing fancy, but it was functional.

"Please, have a seat," she said as she pulled out one of the large leather chairs and sat down. I followed suit.

"Now, let's start from the beginning. I see from these documents that Mr. and Mrs. Charles are petitioning the court for full custody of the minor child Jermaine Charles. He's your son?" she asked. "Yes."

I then spent the next thirty minutes or so explaining the entire situation to her, including the fact that I had written and signed a document in which I agree to have them take care of Jermaine. I explained that I had also agreed to allow them to take Jermaine out of the country for school and that my main concern now was that they would try to send him back to Jamaica and keep him there.

JoAnne was amazing. A strong willed individual who knew her stuff as she immediately reassured me that just because Mr. and Mrs. Charles had money, did not mean that they would be granted custody. She explained that the judge's job was to determine what was best for the child. She also assured me that my asking for help was not a sign of an unfit mother or a sign of weakness, but rather a show of great strength and in fact showed that I was thinking of what was best for my child.

"Now, the first thing we have to do is to ensure that they do not remove Jermaine from the country and send him back to Jamaica," she said. I knew right then that she was exactly what I needed. After some further discussion and providing JoAnne with further details as to how this all came about, I left her office with a sense of hope for the first time since this all began and an even greater determination to fight for Jermaine.

JoAnne was swift in preparing for our court appearance only a few days after our meeting as she recognized the true urgency of my situation.

That morning, I was up at the crack of dawn a complete bundle of nerves as I had never been inside a courtroom before never mind the fact that it was the day that I could lose my prince if the court agreed with the statements of his grandparents that I was 'crazy' and unfit to raise him.

I got out of bed, jumped in the shower and knowing that I had to present a strong presence in the courtroom, I proceeded to put on my black pencil skirt, fuchsia pink blouse, and a wide black belt with gold studs as planned from the night before. Black leather pumps completed my look. I tried to rehearse what I would say to the Judge to make sure he/she knew that I was not unfit and that I was more than capable of raising my son. I thought about what I would do or say when I saw Mr. and Mrs. Charles and if Jermaine would be in the courtroom as his little fate was being determined by a perfect stranger. Would he even understand what was going on? How would this affect him later in life? Would his father be there and what would he have to say, if anything?

The drive to the Brampton Courthouse was short and I found myself pulling into the parking lot much earlier than I expected. I had hoped that the drive would have provided me with the much needed time to gather myself and prepare for what could be the worst day of my life. Instead, I barely had time to recall the details of my agreement with the Charles's as I knew that they would draw heavily on the words contained in that agreement.

I shook it off, put on my game face and exited the car. My stride was quick and steady as I wanted to appear confident and determined, while inside I was scared to death and riddled with doubt. I entered through the doors of the courthouse and was immediately greeted by two court officers in full uniform. I was directed to empty my pockets and to place my purse in the small plastic bin before walking through the metal detector in front of me. I did so as quickly as I could, grabbed my purse out of the plastic bin and headed down the hallway to meet JoAnne whom I prayed was already there. The last thing I wanted was to run into the Charles alone as I had no idea what I would have said to them.

I was very relieved to see JoAnne standing in the hallway directly in front of the courtroom which we entered shortly thereafter. She was sharply dressed as usual. This time in a tailored beige pantsuit and dark brown pumps. She looked all business and ready for a fight.

Her sheer presence and the conviction she exhibited was comforting and helped to boost my confidence in her ability. She greeted me with a reassuring smile and told me that everything would be alright. I believed her. After all, what other choice did I have?

"Time to go," she said as she entered the courtroom, I followed directly behind her and took a seat on the wooden bench to my right. JoAnne walked past the knee-high wall at the front of the room and approached the lady seated in a black leather chair at the large wooden desk with her back facing me. JoAnne then proceeded to remove some documents from her briefcase and handed them to the female. I glanced over to my left to see that Mr. and Mrs. Charles had already arrived and were seated a few rows in front of me to the left. They made no attempt to engage or to look at me. My heart started to race as I glanced to see if Jermaine was seated with them. Thankfully, he was not. He really didn't need to be put through this after what he went through a few nights ago. Cliff was seated in the back of the courtroom to my left and also did not acknowledge me.

The hearing was surprisingly short as the judge took only a few minutes to make his decision after hearing from JoAnne and the Charles's. Cliff was also given an opportunity to speak and chose to support his parents' petition for custody of Jermaine.

The Judge subsequently determined that my actions were not that of an unfit mother but that of someone who recognized her difficulty and took steps to ensure that her child was taken care of. He denied the Charles's petition for custody of Jermaine rewarding me with full custody and court ordered support payments to be made by his father, Cliff. The Charles's were granted the right to have input into

Jermaine's education, which they never did exercise. That only made me wonder about the real reason they wanted custody of my baby. He then went on to order Mr. and Mrs. Charles to return Jermaine to me effective immediately.

I wanted to jump out of my seat, scream out in victory and then throw a few choice words at Cliff and his parents but instead, I chose to take the mature route. Tears of joy flowed freely down my cheeks as I held my head high and revelled in my triumph over the Titans. I won!!!!!

JoAnne explained that I would just have to wait a few minutes for the order to be drawn up and signed and then I was free to go pick up Jermaine. Words cannot explain the gratitude I felt at that moment and to this day for JoAnne's support and particularly her confidence in me.

I left the courthouse that morning on top of the world knowing that Jermaine would be back with me where he belonged. I would never again, let him out of my sight. That afternoon Samantha and I prepared for his return. I ran around the apartment like I had really lost my mind (no pun intended) trying to make sure that the apartment was perfect, his room was spotless and there were snacks in the kitchen. Like a seven- year-old would really care about all that. Except for the snacks of course.

Then it was time to make the drive to Mississauga once again but this would be the last time I ever made the trip to that house. Samantha and I jumped in the car. It was hard to hide my excitement except to give way to my nerves. What if he hates me? What if he really doesn't remember me? What if I made a mistake in fighting for him because I really couldn't be a good mother? Oh, stop it! He loves you, how could he forget his own mother and you'll be a great mother despite what the Charles's think or say. You're right! Let's go get my little prince. Yes. At the risk of sounding 'crazy' I spoke to myself and answered back as well.

We arrived at the house late that afternoon and pulled into the driveway. Samantha and I got out of the car almost simultaneously. She went to open the trunk in anticipation of putting Jermaine's things inside. Me, I tried not to bolt to the door instead settled for a brisk walk to the door trying not to look too smug. I rang the doorbell twice just to make sure that they heard it. A few moments later the door swung open to reveal Mr. Charles standing in the doorway. Jermaine's things were on the floor behind him waiting. Other than a brief acknowledgment of each other, we did not speak. I called out for Jermaine and then saw him emerge at the top of the stairs wearing the biggest smile I've ever seen. I had forgotten how beautiful and white his teeth were. His black dress pants, gray shirt and shiny black leather shoes made him look like a perfect little gentleman. The Charles's always took great pride in his appearance and had a particular style and thoughts of how they want to see him dressed. He was taller too, at least 4 inches or more and had a dark chocolate brown complexion courtesy of the Jamaican sun. He slowly walked towards me and I could see that he was nervous. I pulled him close, picked him up and held him tight. I could feel him relax in my arms and then tightened his arms and legs around me.

Mrs. Charles sat quietly in the family room. I began to pick up Jermaine's things and walked to the car, placing them in the truck. Samantha accompanied me on the second trip to help things move faster. I told Jermaine to go say goodbye to his grandparents and with that he ran into the family room where Mr. Charles had now joined Mrs. Charles. Samantha and I put the final few things in the car while they said their goodbyes. I then retrieved Jermaine from the hallway, scooped him up in my arms, said goodbye to his grandparents and scurried out the door and to the car as if still afraid that he would be taken from me.

It would be years before I would allow his grandparents to see him again, out of fear that they would refuse to return him again. We all needed to heal from the wounds of those events. His father would also remain out his life, failing to pay child support as ordered by the court. It was once again, me and my prince against the world, but that was okay, he was worth it.

A New Beginning

*Second chances are your opportunity
to show that you've made mistakes
and are better because of them.*

March 1992. Another somewhat nice day, you know, not yet warm enough to go without a coat but not near as cold as the winter had just been. The sun was shining and the sky blue which gave the illusion that it was warmer than it actually was. The leafless trees that stood tall in the yard reminded me that summer was still several months away.

With not much else to do that day I decided to hop into my red Dodge Shadow and make the drive to Toronto ON. Having grown up in the suburbs of Mississauga, I had a healthy disdain for driving in the city, but I was still loving the freedom of having my own car so I drove it every chance I got.

Sharon, my older sister, was opening a baby clothing store and needed some help getting the place ready for opening day which wasn't that far away.

The drive there was pretty much what you'd expect at 11:00am on a Saturday morning in a major metropolis. That was until I found myself lost on Allen Rd. I have no idea what went wrong with the directions but I somehow ended up passing the entrance to the small plaza several times. Oh, don't judge! The entrance was quite tricky and for someone who wasn't familiar with the area, almost impossible to find the first time around.

After several attempts, I finally pull up in front of the empty unit and entered through the glass front door. Sharon and her husband David were already there and the preparation of the place was in full swing. Boxes, shelving units and god only knows what else was everywhere. It was clearly an accident waiting to happen.

I got right to work after a short greeting. Without hesitation, Sharon handed me a screwdriver and pointed in the direction of a ladder leaning against the right hand wall. I was tasked to secure the metal tracks that would support the angular rods, on which the clothing would be displayed, to the walls. I had always been handy with tools so this assignment didn't faze me at all.

There, one down only a dozen or so to go. I started my descent down the ladder when out of the corner of my right eye I caught a glimpse of this guy heading out the back door. He had the body of an Adonis, wide shoulders, a small waist, a perfectly rounded butt and massive muscular legs. Breathe!

He wore a tattered dark green and black sweater that hung to one side of his amazing shoulders and faded blue jeans which were quite snug. Not sure how he got into them but my eyes were very appreciative that he made the effort.

David must have seen my eyes wandering to the back entrance

because he blurted out his name; "Greg" before I could even ask the question. "We train together and have been friends forever." By 'train together', I assumed he meant body building, something my brother-in-law as quite into. A short introduction followed once Greg entered the room carrying another large box filled with more stuff. Like we really needed more stuff in that small space, but I didn't mind watching him bend down to place the box on the floor. It was the perfect opportunity for another look at that body and now his symmetrically perfect arms. He stood 5'10" probably 200lbs (all muscle), dark chocolate complexion, dark brown eyes and short black hair with a high-top cut, kind of like Kid n Play, the 80's rap duo.

For the next few hours, Greg made several attempts to make small talk and to convince me to exchange phone numbers. I wasn't ready for that. Way too much going on. With Jermaine away, I was still trying to piece my life together so that I could properly care of him when he returned. So it would be just over a year before I would see Greg again.

After several years of trying to convince Sharon to move to Mississauga the day had finally come. I couldn't believe it. That meant that Jermaine would have the opportunity to get closer to his cousins.

It was a great day to move, not too hot and no rain in sight. As I got ready to make the short drive to their new townhouse all I could think was; the only thing that would make this better is that the move is organized and quick! What are the chances of that? When was the last time you went to help with a house move and it was fast or organized? Wishful thinking never hurt anyone, right?

I arrived at the townhouse complex on Glen Erin Drive and made the left turn into the driveway. After driving around in the maze for a while, I finally pull up to the unit and parked my car on the side of the road just in front of the house. Why do they have to make it so confusing to maneuver through those townhouse complexes?

The front door was open with the screen door propped open to accommodate the constant traffic of people moving in and out with various boxes and pieces of furniture. I was relieved to see that the move was already in progress which meant there was a slim possibility that we would finish before midnight.

"Helloooooo!!!" I yelled in true Elaine form. "Back here" was the reply. I headed to the back area and entered into the kitchen where Sharon was repositioning some boxes on the counter. Several piles of boxes were littered throughout the main floor as though they had just been dumped where ever there was a space on the beige carpeted floor. So, I began the daunting task of sorting the boxes and moving them to their assigned rooms throughout the house while Sharon continued to organize the kitchen.

I had just reached the top of the stairs with a large box marked 'master bedroom' when the loud engine noise of the moving truck backing into the driveway got my attention. Looking out the front bedroom window I saw David exit from the drivers' side of the large white truck followed by a familiar well-built man in faded blue jeans. Even after more than a year how could I forget that frame. Greg, I thought to myself and suddenly I knew that this move was going to be another few hours of small talk with Greg as I try to let him down gently.

As the day progressed, I busied myself with moving as many boxes as possible, then focused on unpacking dishes and various food items and setting up the kitchen with Sharon. "Time for a break!" Thank God because I was about to faint from hunger. In no time the house was filled with the unmistakable aroma of Kentucky Fried Chicken and all work came to an abrupt halt. I helped myself to a paper plate and filled it with chicken, fries and a little coleslaw. Now the question was where to sit. The sliding patio doors off the kitchen offered up a hard but convenient spot on the step leading out to the backyard. I perched myself on the step and began to enjoy my meal. I barely got a few bites in before down sat Greg. Some more small talk followed and then out of nowhere he said "I'm going to marry you one day." I almost choked on my food! I simply looked at him and then excused myself. Needless to say, it wasn't long before I was on my way back home wondering what kind of 'stalker' had I just met.

After several messages from David acting as the middle man for Greg over the next several months, I finally agreed to give Greg a chance, after all, what did I have to lose? Our first date was dinner and a movie. It was a nice evening but to be honest, I wasn't ready to bring someone into our lives.

Our next date would not be for several more months and as they say; "the rest is history." Some would say ours was a whirl-wind romance. Greg was kind, gentle, caring and knew what he wanted. Most importantly, he immediately accepted Jermaine as his own and has continued to this day.

On Valentine's Day 1994, after a beautiful evening out with a group of friends, Greg asked me to marry him after asking Jermaine if it was ok with him, I later discovered. On January 6, 1995, in a small ceremony with family and close friends I married Greg Wilson with Jermaine by my side.

Wow, he actually asked Jermaine if it was ok. Maybe this was exactly what we needed. Does Jermaine need a father figure? Every child needs a father figure, right? And Greg was more than willing to slip into that role and did without hesitation. Greg did the best he could to be there for us, provide for his new family and continued to treat Jermaine as his own flesh and blood.

A new home would follow shortly after our wedding. Things were really coming together and life was good. It was a beautiful brand new four-bedroom end unit townhouse in Brampton with a full wall of windows. Something I had always hoped for and it was now finally a reality. Now Jermaine would have his own backyard, a driveway for a basketball net and an opportunity to meet new friends. Life was promising. All that was missing was a sister or brother for Jermaine. Or was it?

After two heartbreaking miscarriages, Nicole was born in February of 1997 followed by Anthony in January of 1998. My family was now complete and all seemed to be falling into place just as I had hoped. This was my second chance to try this mother thing again and this time maybe I would get it right.

It was comforting to know that this time there would be a strong father figure in their lives from the very beginning. One who would love them unconditionally, support and provide for them from that day on and always. One who'd encourage them to be strong, independent and above all confident. This time, I would not have to do it all alone.

So I began to do things a little different. No longer would it be my goal to give them everything that their little hearts desired but to provide them with what they needed.

As they got older, they too would have specific responsibilities around the house, although I must admit that I still didn't always enforce the expectations. There would continue to be rules around bedtimes, homework, friends, and curfews but this time I spoke with them more about the importance of education, being leaders not followers, choosing friends wisely and staying away from drugs. I also gave them the freedom to develop their own independence instead of totally sheltering them as I did Jermaine. Surely this was what a good mother was supposed do to make sure that her children stayed on the right path. Right?

The Journey Begins

*Raising children will push you to
heights of understanding and patience
you never thought possible.*

My journey through the justice system alongside my first
born began with a soul-shattering phone call at work from a
member of Peel Regional Police. It was the summer of 2000, Jermaine
was barely fifteen and our lives were about to be changed.

"Mrs. Wilson?" "Yes" I responded. "This is Constable Thompson
of the Peel Regional Police," the voice on the other end said. I
immediately began to gather the things on my desk in preparation
to rush out of the building to the nearest hospital to be with one of
my children. Nothing could have prepared me for what he would
say next. "We have your son Jermaine here at 22 Division. He's been
arrested for assault and theft," he said. "We need you to come down
to the station as soon as possible," he continued after a short breath.

My heart stopped, I felt faint, my knees buckled beneath me as
I sank to the floor with the phone receiver still in my hand. With
some effort, I managed to open my mouth and spit out the words
"I'm on my way," I then dropped the phone. I'm not sure if I put the
receiver back on the base or not, all I know was that I was on the
move. I informed whoever I had to that I had a family emergency

and bolted out the door. The next thing I remember was pulling into the parking lot at 22 Division. Good thing I worked close by as I don't remember how I actually got there. I'm sure I must have cut off more than a few people in my panic-fueled drive to the station. I was so distraught that I didn't even think to call Greg, then at home with our younger children, to let him know what was happening.

With tears streaming down both sides of my face, I flew out of the car like a bat out of hell, ran across the parking lot and burst through the double glass doors. It wasn't until all eyes turned and looked in my direction that I realized that I was still in my uniform. Now mortified, as my uniform revealed my employment with the justice system, I approached the front desk and identified myself as Mrs. Wilson. As soon as I stated my name Constable Thompson, who just happened to be passing by, interjected and introduced himself. He then escorted me to the room off to the side where Jermaine was seated with another officer. Constable Thompson explained that Jermaine had gotten into a fight with another youth at a local park. He informed me that the youth had instigated an argument with Jermaine and then struck him. Jermaine then proceeded to hit the youth causing him to fall backwards off the bleachers and onto the ground where Jermaine continued to punch and kick him as he laid on the ground. My first thought was; ok, so the other kid started the fight, Jermaine defended himself and he's the one in custody? How does that make any sense? Constable Thompson further explained that if Jermaine had simply walked away after striking the other youth, it would have been a simple case of self defense. The fact that Jermaine continued to kick and hit the kid while he laid defenseless on the ground is why he was arrested and charged.

The charges were Assault and Theft Under, as the youth alleged that Jermaine had removed a necklace from his neck following the fight. As a mother, my first instinct was to defend my child. I thought to myself, why would Jermaine want anyone else's necklace when he has his own? This just doesn't sound right.

Constable Thompson picked up some papers off the desk and then proceeded to flip through the pages while explaining to me that Jermaine would be released into my custody, however, he would need to return to the station the next day at 9:00am to be fingerprinted and photographed. He then pointed out a few areas that I needed to sign. I gladly signed where indicated as all I wanted to do was to get Jermaine out of that place.

After verbally promising to return to have his fingerprints and photos taken the next morning, to appear in Youth Court on the date indicated, and also signing the papers, Jermaine was released into my care.

Still in total shock, leaving the station, I said nothing to Jermaine as I feared the wrong thing would come out of my mouth. The fifteen-minute ride home was silent and gave me time to think. A million thoughts trampled through my brain. Now, what? How could this have happened? Oh, God please don't let him have to go to jail! With everything in me, I wanted to protect him from that experience as I knew it would change his life forever. I couldn't even entertain that thought, so I quickly pushed it out of my mind. How do I go back to work? Who can I talk to about this without my business getting spread all over the place? Given my line of work, I had to at least tell my manager as there was a possibility of a conflict of interest with even the slightest possibility that Jermaine could be found guilty and sentenced to custody.

Jermaine and I spoke briefly about what happened when we got home. He explained that he didn't start the fight, that he only fought back, and that he was confused why he was being charged. He adamantly denied stealing the necklace and stated that it broke off during the scuffle. I believed him because he was my son and at that point, he had no reason to lie.

The next morning, I awoke bright and early then got Jermaine out of bed. We drove to the police station, arriving early as I tend to do, leaving Greg at home with Nicole and Anthony. I approached the desk, identified myself and informed the officer that I had brought Jermaine to have his fingerprints and photograph taken. She politely asked us to sit in the waiting area until his name was called. I walked to a seat furthest from the door and away from the desk, Jermaine followed. I was terrified that someone I knew would walk through the front door. The last thing I wanted to do was to explain my presence there to anyone.

A few minutes later a female officer exited the room to our left. "Jermaine Charles." she said and with that we both rose from our seats and headed in her direction. She quickly informed me that I could not accompany Jermaine into the room however, I could watch from outside the door. I stood helplessly watching my baby boy being treated like a common criminal. I watched as she took each finger pressed them onto the ink pad and then transferred his fingerprint onto a piece of paper and then instructed him to stand still against the wall as she took his photograph. I was heartbroken, never in my wildest dreams did I picture myself in this position. Nor did I expect to witness my child go through this process. A process that I myself had put many through over the years as a requirement of my job. It certainly gave me a different perspective; humbled me, you might say.

That afternoon I went on the hunt for a lawyer who would take care of my prince. My first thought was JoAnne who I remembered also practiced Criminal Law. She had done such a great job during my fight for custody that I had every confidence that she would be the one to handle this situation.

Where on earth was I going to find her number after all these years? That was a number I never anticipated ever needing again. Was I going to be one of those people who needed a lawyer on speed dial and retainer? I certainly hope not.

After looking in a few obvious places for the number to no avail, I picked up the phone and dial 411. "A business number for JoAnne Winters, Lawyer," I said to the automated voice on the other end. After a minute or so I was provided with the number and hung up the phone. I quickly dialed the number while trying to think of what I was going to say. I was embarrassed, not sure why but I dreaded the judgment that would most likely come my way. I felt like a child who was going to tell her parents about something wrong they had done. Get a grip Elaine! She's a lawyer. Not your mother or your friend! You're a grown woman with children, get a grip!

"JoAnne Winters' office." I was startled by the person on the other end as I was still caught up in the thoughts running through my head. "Hi, my name is Elaine Wilson and I need to speak with JoAnne as soon as possible." "Miss Winters is in court at the moment. I will ask her to give you a call later this evening," the polite but young sounding voice responded. After providing her with my contact information and thanking her for her time, I slowly hung up the phone. To tell you the truth, I was a little relieved that JoAnne was unavailable. That gave me a few hours to gather my thoughts rather than the few seconds I had just experienced while waiting for the call to be answered.

Around 6:00pm that evening the phone rang. I reluctantly picked up the receiver.

"May I speak with Elaine Wilson?" the friendly sounding voice with a slight English accent said.

"Speaking."

"This is JoAnne Winters, how are you Elaine?" she said as if familiar with who I was. "How's Jermaine doing?"

Wow, she did actually remember who I was. That really helped to put me at ease and reinforced that I had made the right decision to call her, but it also made it more difficult to inform her as to why I was calling.

"Well, Jermaine is why I'm actually calling. He's been charged with Assault and Theft. He got into a fight with some kid in the park yesterday." I explained.

"Is he being held in custody?"

"No. He was released to me at the police station."

"Good. When is his court appearance?"

She was all business, no judgment just focused. I liked that. I retrieved the papers I got from Constable Thompson and read the information to JoAnne.

"Okay, so we need to get together to discuss the details as soon as possible. Let's see. Tomorrow is no good as I'm in court all day. Ok, how about the day after around 3:00pm?"

"We'll be there."

"Good. See you then. There will be a retainer of $1000. Can you do that?" She asked.

"We'll figure it out. See you at three. Thank you, JoAnne."

"You're welcome. See you soon. In the meantime, try not to worry. Everything will be fine."

"Thanks again."

With that, I hung up the phone feeling somewhat relieved that Jermaine was in good hands.

Greg and I made the drive to JoAnne's office in virtual silence. There wasn't much to say actually because we're both the type of people who would rather run scenarios through our heads than speak of them aloud. Maybe it was our way of not making them too real. Plus, I was ashamed to really speak of the situation because although Greg had never treated Jermaine as if he was not his child, I felt that Jermaine was my sole responsibility and did not want to put that kind of burden on him. Not that he would have mind, but that was just me.

For days I cried, too embarrassed, ashamed and now feeling guilty for having failed Jermaine, so I told no one what had really happened.

Greg and I did not speak of Jermaine's situation. I began to feel that Jermaine's behavior was my failure, my responsibility and had nothing to do with Greg. After all, I had raised him on my own for the first ten years of his life and should have taught him all he needed to know about making the right choices. It became easier to internalize all the feelings of shame, embarrassment and guilt, slowly eating away at my soul than to admit out loud that I had failed. Greg did the best he could to stand by my side and by Jermaine but he stayed silent and eventually distant. I'm not sure if it was to give me the space I seem to have wanted or because I began to withdraw into myself. I was overwhelmed with fear of having another depressive episode, so I kept him at arms-length, choosing to deal with Jermaine on my own.

JoAnne was amazing, as usual. She was easy to speak to. It was as though we were good friends. She spoke without judgment and then assured us that things would be okay. Jermaine's court appearance followed shortly after our first meeting. This courthouse is getting a little too familiar, I thought as I arrived at the same Brampton Courthouse where once again Jermaine's fate was in the hands of a total stranger but this time in Criminal Court. This court appearance was short as JoAnne requested another court date in order to prepare Jermaine's defense. Several weeks later I received a call from JoAnne informing us that the charges had been down-graded, Jermaine would be placed on one year probation and would have to do 30 community service hours.

I remember thinking that the ordeal was over and that we had all came through it in one piece. Was it and did we?

Little did I realize that this was just the beginning....

Tough Love

*Sometimes the best plan is simply
knowing when it's time to try
something new.*

Several months later Jermaine would be charged again.

Right under my nose, Jermaine had slowly transformed into someone I did not recognize. First skipping class, then skipping school altogether. I soon discovered that he was smoking marijuana. It went from there to missed curfews, then to not coming home at all for days at a time. I was frantic not knowing where he was or if he was okay, but I never thought it would come to this. Maybe I spent too much time trying to be a better mother, this time around, with Anthony and Nicole and missed the signs of Jermaine's pain which surely must have been there. Maybe I could have prevented Jermaine's journey down this road that would only lead to self-destruction if I was paying more attention. All the maybes in the world couldn't erase what had been happening and I was at a total loss as to what to do next to help him see that his choices were only going to lead to more encounters with the law.

This time, I was awakened by a call in the mid-afternoon after working a night shift. The voice on the other end of the line sounded vaguely familiar as I struggled to bring myself to consciousness.

"Mrs. Wilson?"

"Speaking. How can I help you?"

"This is Daniel Samuels a Social Worker at the Toronto Youth Assessment Centre."

Suddenly, my recollection of how I knew this voice came rushing back. Daniel and I worked together only a few years earlier.

"I have your son Jermaine here with me in the office, he was brought in earlier charged with possession of narcotics with intent to sell. He has a bail hearing scheduled for tomorrow and he wanted to see if you would be there in court."

My shock quickly turned to pure anger, frustration and disappointment. How could this be happening again? What was he thinking? I can't do this again. OMG, who else knows he's there and that he's my son? What does this mean for me at work? My worst nightmare had come true. Jermaine was in the last place I ever wanted him to be. What do I do now? Get him out as soon as possible? Leave him there in hopes that this is an opportunity for him to learn first-hand that he doesn't belong in a place like that? I struggled with these thoughts. Suddenly, my mouth opened, I closed off a large part of my heart and informed Daniel that I would not be in court and that maybe it would be beneficial to Jermaine if he were to spend the weekend there.

It was the hardest decision I have ever had to make. No mother, especially one with the inside knowledge of that environment, ever wants to have to make the decision to leave her child in custody, but I truly felt that I had no choice at that point. Obviously, his first brush with the law wasn't enough to show him that he was so much better than the choices he was making. He was still young and it wasn't too late. I wasn't about to lose my child to the system, so it was time to go the "scared straight" route. Maybe seeing what it's really like in there would open his eyes to his true and full potential. Hopefully, he would get to see that it's not the glamorous life that some tend to paint it to be. So I prayed.

In shock at my response, Daniel asked if I was sure that was what I wanted to do. Of course, it wasn't what I wanted to do, it was what I felt I had to do. The "tough love" method was my last ditch effort to turn Jermaine around.

This approach failed miserably and it was clear that I had not been as good a teacher as I thought and once again my parenting methods had failed. I had to come to terms with the fact that regardless of what I did or said, I was not Jermaine's only influence. Despite his past brush with the law, something/someone out there was still driving him on the road to destruction.

My decision tore our family apart and sadly, Jermaine disappeared from our lives after being bailed out by someone unknown to me, staying with friends and eventually going to live with his father for periods of time.

What I didn't know then, was that Jermaine was torn between two lives. The life of the quiet, respectful, and well-mannered child I knew and the rebellious teenager I had recently been exposed to. I eventually came to realize that his behavior outside of our home was in some way his suit of armor, a kind of protection or survival suit, if you may, in order for him to fit into his teenage world. A world I did not know nor could I have ever understood. A world that would eventually take hold of my child, altering the course of his life forever.

It would be several years before we would see each other again despite my attempts to have him return home. During that time, it was rumored that there were more charges and several court appearances resulting in various probation orders.

Not a day went by that I didn't pray for him; wonder where he was and if he was ok. I prayed that wherever he was, he always felt my presence and never doubted my love for him. My heart sank every time my phone rang, hoping that this wasn't the call that would inform me that I had lost my prince forever.

Thank God that call never came. Jermaine slowly re-entered our lives, by then an adult in his early twenties. By all accounts, he remained the polite, well-mannered son I had raised and I continued to pray that he had left that life behind and was ready to move on with the life I had always dreamed of for him.

Still, I questioned; Had I really given Jermaine all he needed to become a confident and responsible adult? Did I teach him to make the right choices in difficult situations or did I shelter him too much? Did I fail to expose him to some of the cruel realities of the world because I knew them all too well? By trying to keep him safe, did I drive him to the very thing I was terrified he'd find?

I realize now that it takes an incredible amount of personal strength and conviction to always pull in the right direction when everyone and everything else is pulling you in the opposite one. Yet, we expect a teenager to accomplish this feat while dealing with all the other physiological changes they go through at that age. I can only say, keep pulling them back no matter how much they resist. The disdain they feel for you now is minimal compared to the disdain you will feel for yourself if you don't. I obviously didn't pull hard enough and for that, I continue to wear the blame as a badge of shame and as a reminder of my failure.

Should I have allowed Greg to play a more aggressive role in Jermaine's rearing? Maybe. Although Greg had openly accepted Jermaine as his own, a large part of me still felt that he was my responsibility. After all, he was my prince and it was supposed to be "me and him against the world." So I continued to keep Greg at bay when it came to Jermaine.

The many sleepless nights, the silence between us and my determination to take on all of the blame and responsibility for my child's behavior, despite having Greg in my life, began to seep into our marriage. Slowly, I began to avoid my responsibilities as a wife, withdrew into myself and spent excessive amount of hours at work. Greg was patient and understanding, but my behavior took its toll.

In November of 2010, I walked away from my marriage of fifteen years as feelings of failure, extreme anguish and worthlessness began to eat away at my ability to be a wife. I no longer felt that I was capable of loving Greg and we progressively grew apart. We vowed to remain as good friends and took great care to ensure that the impact on the kids would be as minimal as the breakup of a family could be for any child. We agreed to shared custody and to live in close proximity to each other so that Nicole and Anthony, now thirteen and twelve years old, would be able to easily move between our two homes and to remain in the neighborhood they were accustomed to so as not to disrupt their relationships with friends and school.

They seemed to adjust to the breakup well and Greg and I did our best to maintain a sense of family despite now living separate lives. But was that enough?

Déjà-vu

If the first time's the test, is the second time simply fate?

Well, can I tell you now that my new approach in parenting also failed? Once again I began to feel like an epic failure when my youngest son Anthony, shortly after his fifteenth birthday, also began his journey through the justice system with me along for the ride as the unseen victim of circumstance.

In March of 2013, what started as another typical day at work soon took an unexpected turn for the absolute worst when that damn phone rang. The call display read 'unknown number'. That's never good.

I picked up the receiver. "Elaine speaking," I said. "Mrs. Wilson?" the voice on the other end asked in a very official sounding voice. The hairs on my arms stood up and a chill consumed my body. "Yes, how can I help you?" I answered with much hesitation in my voice.

"This is Constable Peters with the Peel Regional Police," he said. I wanted to just hang up the phone because I really didn't want to hear what was coming next. My heart leaped into my throat and tears began to well up in my eyes just waiting for permission to start running down my face. What happened to Jermaine this time? Was this the phone call I was waiting for? I really wanted to believe that he had turned his life around. Please tell me he's ok. I thought to myself because not even in my wildest dreams could I have imagined that he was calling about Anthony. Not after I had done everything right this time.

"We have your son Anthony down at 22 Division. He's been arrested for Assault" he said. I can't even begin to accurately explain how I felt. Let's see. Start by taking a hot knife, insert it slowly into your stomach and twist it repeatedly. Maybe now you might just have a glimpse of how I felt.

The pain was intolerable. Those feelings of guilt, failure, disappointment in myself and inadequacy all came rushing back like a tsunami towards the shore. This was surely definitive proof that I was never meant to be a mother and that I should have never been given that privilege. Another life ruined at my hand, I thought.

I hung up the phone and immediately called Greg to let him know what happened and to tell him that I was heading to the police station. I then managed to pull myself together just enough to once again made that dreaded phone call to my Deputy to inform her that I had a family emergency and had to leave work immediately. I ran out of the building barely holding the tears back, got into my car and made the ten-minute drive to 22 Division. This was becoming way too familiar.

With blood shot eyes, I entered the police station and approached the constable sitting behind the desk. She was polite and helpful. I think that was in part because of my uniform. I gave her my name and told her that I had received a call from Constable Peters about my son Anthony. She instructed me to have a seat and pointed to her right. The station was quite busy with limited space to sit so I stood by the back door using every bit of energy I had to hold back the tears. I looked over to the front door just as Greg was walking through it. Almost like I had sensed his arrival. I motioned to him to join me and tried to stand strong, holding my composure the best I could by not embracing him. I knew that if I had allowed his embrace I would have immediately fallen to pieces and Anthony needed my strength.

About five minutes later we were approached by Constable Peters, who introduced himself and apologized for having to call me at work. He then informed me that Anthony had requested to see me and then motioned for me to follow him as he walked to the room in the back area. Something I had done several years earlier with Jermaine.

This time was different, I expected to see Anthony as I turned the corner but instead I was met by another officer who informed me that Anthony was being held in the prisoner's area downstairs. Just the word 'prisoner' sent chills down my spine. He couldn't be talking about my child.

Constable Peters explained that it was reported that Anthony and two other boys had gotten into a fight with another boy in the parking lot of a local community centre. He stated that Anthony matched the description of one of the boys the victim described in the assault.

I asked Constable Peters if I could see him. He explained to me that they did not usually allow the public downstairs. Recognizing my uniform and as a professional courtesy, he informed me that he would speak to his supervisor. He then picked up the phone and after a brief conversation returned the receiver to the base. I guess his supervisor had been close by because within seconds, another officer appeared. Sergeant Williams introduced himself and then agreed to take me to see Anthony. He escorted me through what appeared to be a metal door and down the stairs where I saw Anthony seated at a small table in an interview room. I was relieved that I did not have to see him in a cell as I knew that would have been a vision that would remain with me forever. Sergeant Williams unlocked the door and I immediately entered the room, wrapped my arms tightly around Anthony and held him close. I then sat down at the table beside him. He appeared surprisingly calm and somewhat emotionless. Anthony was never one to show a lot of emotion. Constable Peters sat next to us. He started off by explaining that this interview would be recorded. He then proceeded to read Anthony his rights and asked if he understood. This was followed by a review of the accusations against him. Throughout the interview Anthony stated that he was not present during the alleged incident. Constable Peters was not content with Anthony's statements as he continued to repeat his questions, I guess in hopes that Anthony would make some sort of admission. That was not the case.

At the end of the interview, Constable Peters informed Anthony that he would be released into my custody. He then informed me that I would have to sign the release papers once they were ready and then I was free to take Anthony home. I was then escorted out of the room and back upstairs to the waiting area where Greg was anxiously awaiting my return. I immediately threw my arms around him and broke down in tears. Not knowing if these were tears of joy or of anguish, Greg also began to weep. I quickly informed Greg that Anthony would be released as soon as we signed some documents and then returned to the back room area to await the paperwork. A few short minutes later, Anthony was standing by my side. Constable Peters reviewed the papers with Anthony, Greg and myself and after a few signatures he was released in our care promising to appear in court on the date indicated. I was then handed Anthony's personal belongings in a small plastic bag.

Anthony repeatedly proclaimed his innocence the entire drive home stating that he wasn't even there. We spoke about his choice of friends and how easy it was to get caught up in things just because of who you're known to associate with. Also about how quickly people will throw your name around in order to save their own skin.

Here we go again. I find myself in need of a lawyer who would help to prove my child's innocence. JoAnne was out of the question this time as I was much too embarrassed to let her know that I had another child who had become involved with the law. So I turned to Jermaine, given his history with the legal system I had also come to learn that he had an extremely good lawyer. So that night I contacted Jermaine and explained Anthony's situation and asked for his lawyer's name and contact information. Jermaine seemed genuinely concerned and disappointed with Anthony's situation and gladly provided me with his lawyer's name and number. He also offered to reach out to his lawyer and explain the situation prior to my contact. How were we going to afford a lawyer? Somehow we had to figure it out and that we did. No one thinks that this is what they would dip into their savings for but we were one of the lucky ones who had that option. Many do not.

A few days later, Greg and I met with Cathy, the lawyer referred by Jermaine, to discuss our options to deal with Anthony's situation. Despite what I thought was a poor presentation, Cathy appeared extremely confident and had a great reputation, so we therefore retained her services putting the fate of our baby boy in her hands. After all, we weren't looking for a friend, we were looking for someone who would go before the court and fight for our child as if he were her own. She had that drive.

Cathy did not let us down. We were extremely relieved when, within a few months and after two court appearances, all charges were dropped. The court had determined that Anthony was in fact not present during the assault.

Maybe I wasn't a total failure as a mother after all. With that, a glimmer of my confidence raised its head, only to be shattered several months later when I received yet another phone call. This time from Greg. "Anthony has been arrested and charged with Breaking and Entering." It was alleged that Anthony and a few of his friends had attempted to climb through the basement window of a home in a nearby neighborhood. Greg informed me that he was at the police station where Anthony was being held, along with the two other youths and their parents.

I couldn't believe what I was hearing and once again prayed that this too was a mistake. I'm not sure how much more of this I can take.

It appeared that Anthony too, seemed to have transformed into someone that I did not recognize. He was usually a quiet and well-mannered with a strong will, much like myself. So it surprised me that he would allow himself to be caught up in that type of situation with his 'friends', given his last experience with 'friends' and the law.

Was this also my fault? Was this Anthony's way of protesting Greg and I's breakup?

Anthony was held at the station overnight and taken to court for a bail hearing the following morning, while the other accused were released into the custody of their parents. I'm sure this was in part because of Anthony's previous involvement with the law. Needless to say, I did not sleep that night. To say that the thought of my baby boy in a holding cell was heartbreaking is a massive understatement. That evening, I placed yet another call to Cathy asking for her help. The following morning Greg and I met Cathy at the Brampton Courthouse as she negotiated the terms of Anthony's release and our bank account took another hit.

After much negotiating with the Crown Attorney, it was agreed that Anthony would be granted bail with several conditions which included a non- association order with the other accused. We knew that this would be no easy feat as Anthony and one of the other accused were extremely close and attended the same school. After showing that we were financially capable to act as sureties and assuring the judge that we were willing and able to enforce the conditions of his bail including accommodating Anthony court appearances, we signed the documents and brought Anthony home.

Again, Anthony repeatedly claimed his innocence, stating that although he was present, he did not enter or attempt to enter the home and in fact was not even on the property. I now realized that the influences of those outside the home were far stronger than we knew and Anthony's ability to resist or walk away was constantly being challenged. I felt unprepared to help him. What was I supposed to do, lock him in the basement?

I spoke to Anthony to ensure that he totally understood the importance of following the conditions set out in his bail and reminded him of the consequences should he fail to do so and we again spoke about the friends he chose to hang out with.

Should I have been more forceful in forbidding him to hang out with those friends? Maybe, but in my experience that only pushed them away from me and into the arms of the 'enemy'. Instead, I pointed out the fact that his 'friends' all slept in their beds last night and that he was the only one in a cell.

Then the wait began again as we prepared for several court appearances, added financial strain and the possible outcome of this new charge. What were the chances that the charges would be dropped again? Without sounding negative and wanting with all my heart to believe in my child, I had to convince myself that that's exactly what would happen.

Several weeks later I received a frantic call at work from Anthony. When I picked up the phone, all I could hear was: "Mom, they're going to take me! Come quick!! Mom, please they're going to take me!" I immediately recognize the voice as Anthony's and I knew from the tone of his voice that something had gone terribly wrong at school.

I dropped the phone and took off out of my office across the field and through the front door, jumped in my car and flew down the road. I was literally blinded by all the thoughts of what could have happened racing through my mind. The fifteen-minute drive to Anthony's school seemed like forever when in fact I was there in just under ten minutes. I pulled up in the front of the school, jumped out of the car leaving it in the school bus zone. I'm not even sure if I turned it off.

As I entered the main office, I was immediately led into the principal's office where Anthony and two police officers along with the principal stood awaiting my arrival. The officers explained to me that Anthony would be charged for breaching the conditions of his bail specifically the non-association order. They informed me that Anthony was seen speaking with his co-accused in the school hallway. After some further discussion and several attempts by Anthony to explain his actions, I was asked to walk with Anthony through the hallway along with the two police officers and out into the parking lot. Upon exiting the school, I immediately saw the police cruiser parked by the side door. One officer asked Anthony to lean on the car and place his hands behind his back; he then placed handcuffs on my baby's wrists.

As much as I try to hold my composure, the site of Anthony in handcuffs was too much to bear and the tears began to freely flow down my face. The officers informed me that they would be taking him to 22 Division and I was to meet them there. Now totally broken, I helplessly watched as the cruiser pulled out of the school parking lot with my baby boy in the back seat. I ran to my car and called Greg to inform him of the situation, then took off to the police station. It seems that luck was again on our side, as Anthony was again released into our custody.

After several court appearances for bail and to set dates for appearances, countless prayers and the amazing negotiation skills of Cathy, Anthony was given the option to complete 50 volunteer hours. This allowed him to avoid a trial and a possible finding of guilt.

We were once again in the clear. I prayed that Anthony would count his blessings just as I did and shift his life in a positive direction.

The Biggest Test of All

Just when you think you have nothing left, you're forced to find that little bit extra.

July 2014. The day started just as many other work day, I arrived at work just before 8:00am in order to get settled in and ready for the first meeting of the day at 9:00am. I got into my office about 8:10am and pushed the 'on' button for my computer. The screen began to illuminate and Windows began to load. As always, there's a lot to do at the start of my shift, and the ringing of the phone was no surprise. I casually picked up the receiver, "Elaine speaking.". The vaguely familiar voice on the other end repeated my name; "Elaine?" "Speaking." I repeated. I immediately recognized the voice as Cliff's. Why on earth was he calling me at work? I didn't even know that he had my work number. This can't be good. Without warning, I heard, "Jermaine's in jail! You need to be at Finch court in Toronto by 9:00am today for his bail hearing. This time, it sounds serious. He's been charged with Human Trafficking." The phone fell from my hand and onto the desk as I fell to my knees. No! not my baby! Not again! I screamed to myself. There must be some mistake! He would never be involved in something like that!" Of course the words 'Human Trafficking' brought a vision of girls travelling in the back of a van and being held at some unidentified location to be later sold to the highest bidder, as in a television scene, came to mind. As strange as it may sound, I would have rather heard that he had been charged with some drug related offence than that. Not that any charge would be acceptable.

I gathered enough composure to dial the extension for my Supervisor. "Francis speaking" the voice on the other end of the line stated. "Francis, I have to leave," was all I managed to get out before the tears began to rush down my face. I'm not even sure what else I said or if I even made sense through my fits of tears, but I hung up the phone, grabbed some things off my desk, wiped the tears from my face and quickly left the area and headed out the door.

Francis must have sensed the panic in my voice because halfway across the field I saw her heading in my direction. As soon as she reached me, my knees buckled and I literally fell into her arms as she struggled to support me. She placed her right arm around my torso trying to support my literally dead weight as we made our way to the front entrance.

"Elaine, what's going on?"

"My son's in jail. He's been arrested and I need to get to court. He's my baby, I can't lose him! Not like this."

"Oh my God, Elaine! What can I do?"

"Nothing. I just need to get there as soon as possible. His bail hearing is at 9:00am at Finch court in Toronto."

We moved as quickly as possible, trying to hide my appearance so as not to arouse the curiosity of my peers.

As we reached the front door, we were greeted by another one the managers who accompanied us to the front of the building. Both of them informed me that they could not allow me to drive in my current state and asked if I had someone that I could call to pick me up and take me to the courthouse. If not one of them would drive me there. As thoughtful as that was, there was no way in hell that I was going to let that happen. I was already mortified about the whole situation and terrified as to how I would be judged if they were to find out the details of his charges. Endless attempts to convince them that I would be okay failed. I eventually got hold of my younger sister Yvonne and then my friend Jen. Yvonne agreed to pick me up at work, but could not take me all the way to Toronto as she had an appointment that she could not miss. Instead she would drop me home where Jen would then pick me up and take me to the courthouse in Toronto. Francis remained by my side until Yvonne arrived to take me home.

The ride was sombre as I was still digesting the unbelievable turn of events. I silently prayed that it was all a huge mistake. Yvonne asked very few questions as I'm sure she saw the fear and devastation on my face. Jen sat waiting in her car with the engine running when we pulled up in front of my house. I quickly thanked Yvonne for the ride and told her that I would call her later when I knew more about what was going on. I jumped out of the car and into Jen's completely forgetting that I was still in uniform. We took off down the road knowing that it was still rush hour and we would have to contend with the 'parking lot' better known as Highway 410.

I was barely in the car before I started to cry again. This is it, I thought, this is the day that no mother ever wants to imagine and dreads none the less. The day that I may have to watch my child (my first born) be carted off by the police and incarcerated. I had to give my head a good shake to get that debilitating picture out of my mind. Instead, I started to pray that he would at least be granted bail while this obvious misunderstanding was sorted out.

When we pulled into the parking lot of the courthouse, my first thought was that it didn't look much like a courthouse, not the traditional building that you see on television dramas. It was located in a strip mall type complex. The big beige coloured, multi-storey building seemed cold and uninviting, I guess that was on purpose. I don't even think that I saw a sign other than the address number on the side which verified that I was in the right place.

Jen pulled her minivan into the first available parking space and asked if I wanted her to stay with me. I immediately thanked her for the drive and told her that I would be okay and that I'm sure I would be able to get a ride home from someone. I had no idea what I was walking into and wanted to spare Jermaine the embarrassment of having a virtual stranger present while he went through what may prove to be the most difficult day of his life. Never mind me wanting to hide my own feelings of shame of having failed him so miserably once again.

As I exited the van, I saw Kelly, (Jermaine's girlfriend) who appeared to be pacing in the parking lot. The distress on her face only increased my anxiety as I approached her. With tears welled up in her eyes, she simply embraced me in support. She looked as though someone had plunged a knife into her heart. Anyone could tell that she was using every ounce of strength in her to fight back the tears and, my guess, the anger she must have been feeling. I must say that I gained a whole new level of respect for her that day as she stood firm in her support of Jermaine. "No matter what, we are bringing Jermaine home with us today," she said with incredible conviction in her voice and then informed me that both her parents were there and were willing to put up whatever amount of money needed to ensure that Jermaine was granted bail. How many women would ask their parents to bail out their boyfriend never mind one charged with Human Trafficking? None that I know of.

My body was overcome with a feeling of relief, yet the tears began to flow down my face as my own inability to financially support Jermaine in his greatest time of need overwhelmed me. I had no idea how much the bail was going to be but I knew it was going to be substantial and much more than I could afford given the seriousness of the charges. Until that day, I had not yet met Kelly's parents although she had been with Jermaine for several years. All I knew was that they were God-sent. How many parents would be willing to post bail for their daughter's boyfriend? To be honest, I'm not sure that I would be able to, but I was and still am extremely grateful that they were. My faith in humanity and the capacity of the human heart was rebuilt that day.

Kelly and I slowly walked, in silence, across the parking lot to the Swiss Chalet restaurant beside the courthouse. Everyone had gathered there for some preliminary discussion with Jermaine's lawyer, Cathy, prior to going into court. We entered the Swiss Chalet and I immediately saw Cathy and my nephew David Jr. sitting with a few others at a table to my right.   We approached the two tables where I said "hello" to David and Cathy. Kelly then introduced me to her parents. I graciously shook their hands as it was the first time we had met, then lowered my head in shame. What I really wanted to do was to grab hold of them both in an unbreakable embrace which couldn't even begin to express how grateful I was that they were there.

Cathy, with her usual abruptness, simply nodded to acknowledge my presence and then began discussing the scope of the charges and what we were possibly facing. I overlooked her demeanor as I knew that she was an amazing attorney with, sadly enough, a history of representing Jermaine.

She began talking about human trafficking, promoting prostitution and assault amongst several other charges. The words flowed out of her mouth casually as if she was ordering a cup of coffee. With every word, I felt a part of my soul die to the point where I felt as though I would either throw up, burst into uncontrollable crying, or simply pass out. Fortunately, I did none of the above.

I simply sat and listened as she outlined what was going to happen when we entered the courtroom and questioned us as to our ability to show that we had the funds available to post the ridiculous amount of bail (in the tens of thousands of dollars) being requested by the Crown Attorney. A feeling of total helplessness came over me when I finally allowed myself to hear the actual amount, knowing that I could not afford that kind of money.

Surely these virtual strangers were not willing to put up that kind of money to help my son. If not, how was I ever going to walk out of that courtroom? I knew that I couldn't leave Jermaine behind knowing that he would be held in an Adult Detention Centre, possibly until the trial. Given the seriousness of the allegations against him and the back-log of cases in our courts, it could be years.

I quickly thought back to the words Kelly had shared with me in the parking lot. "My parents are willing to put up whatever amount of money to ensure that Jermaine is granted bail." Then, like music to my ears, I heard Kelly's parents confidently assure Cathy that they would assume the responsibility of Surety for Jermaine's bail. Cathy then broke down the numbers with us so that we all understood what we were about to do. Kelly's parents would assume 90% of the financial responsibility, myself and one of Jermaine's friends would assume the remaining 10%.

What does someone say to that kind of selflessness? How do you thank someone for such incredible gestures of kindness? As long as I live, I will never be able to repay such an enormous debt.

Shortly after, the cell phone sitting on the table in front of Cathy rang signaling that it was time for us to report to courtroom 208. We all filed out of the restaurant one behind the other and approached the gloomy looking building in which I was about to learn my child's fate. I walked through the glass door which opened upon my approach revealing a small area manned by two special constables of the Metro Toronto Police. I placed my red purse in the small plastic bin along with my cell phone and the earpiece which I removed from my right ear. The court officer standing to my right immediately picked up the plastic bin with its contents and placed it on the conveyor belt to run it through the x-ray machine. With a stern and authoritative voice, the other officer looked at me and instructed me to remove anything from my pockets. Although I was certain that my pockets were empty, I went through the motion of placing my hands in each pocket and slowly removed them revealing nothing in my hands in order to satisfy his curiosity.

He then motioned for me to walk through the metal detector towards him which I did. The detector made a low-key beep as I passed through. I suppose it was caused by my belt or the watch on my left hand because I was certain that I had nothing else that would have set it off.

He immediately raised his two arms out to his side one of which held a small black device with a yellow label (a search wand). I knew right away as it was similar to the ones we use at work when searching the youth in our custody. I mimicked his actions stretching both my arms out away from my side. He slowly approached me and moved the wand across my chest, down both of my out-stretched arms, up and down my torso and then down the front of both legs. "Turn around" he instructed, I complied. He then moved the wand up and down my back and down the back of both legs to my ankles. "Go ahead," he said as he used his right hand to motion me in the right direction.

I collected my purse, cell phone and earpiece from the plastic bin and followed the others down the wide hallway which stretched out in front of me. I slowly walked through the hallway scanning both sides hoping that I wouldn't see any of my past clients. Cathy led the way and came to a stop in front of courtroom 208. There were a few small metal benches with blue cushioned seats secured to the floor in a small waiting area just outside the doors leading into the courtroom. I approached the bench and sat nervously beside Kelly. Cathy went in through the large wooden doors and disappeared into the courtroom leaving us all seated in the hallway. A few short minutes later she popped her head out and summoned us to the courtroom. Here we go, I thought to myself as I reluctantly got up from my seat and followed the others through the large wooden doors.

To my surprise, the room was quite small. The cherry coloured wooden benched on both sides were already partially occupied. Directly in front was a large cherry wood platform were the judge would soon sit to hear the particulars of the cases before him. A coat of arms hung prominently on the wall behind his bench. Several other courtroom staff were milling around engaged in various conversations. Cathy sat in the chair behind a small desk on the right side of the courtroom facing the judge's bench. A tired looking woman with dirty blonde hair, a slight build, wearing black pants a rose coloured blouse, black jacket and brown loafers, hurried into the room. She quickly took her place behind the desk on the left hand side of the room facing the judge's bench, carrying a large stack of files and looking as though she was late for an event. I assumed, she was the Crown Attorney. She looked like a woman on a mission and that worried me somewhat as she did not appear that she was in the business of compromise. Cathy got up from her seat and briefly spoke with her. I wondered what they were saying, but couldn't hear the conversation. I know it had something to do with us as she looked over at us as Cathy spoke. It must be about our intention to act as Jermaine's sureties.

Suddenly all was quiet in the courtroom except for the gentleman who loudly said "ALLLL RISE!" and with that, everyone in the courtroom stood up from their seats. The judge entered through a door at the front of the room to the left of his bench and took his seat behind the bench overlooking the courtroom. He was a miserable looking older gentleman with salt and pepper hair, dressed in a black robe with the white collar displayed on the outside. Oh great, another one who looks like they are just not in the mood today, I thought. Boy, I hope this is one of those times when looks are really deceiving.

We sat quietly as the Crown Attorney rummaged through the large stack of files she had entered with. One after the other the court clerk called out names, waited for the representing attorneys to respond and present their clients before the court. Charges were read aloud and bail or variations of current bail orders were granted. Things might not be that bad after all. No one's been denied bail or a bail variation so far, I though.

"Jermaine Charles!" I held my breath in anticipation of seeing Jermaine enter the courtroom. No response. "Jermaine Charles!" she repeated, this time, a little louder and with more authority in her voice. The court clerk then picked up the phone on her desk and started to speak. I could see her mouth moving, but I couldn't hear her voice. I assumed that she was calling downstairs to the court cells to ensure that Jermaine was being brought up.

A few minutes later, a handcuffed Jermaine was ushered into the courtroom through a door to my left by two court officers. One of the officers opened the small door which led to the 'prisoners box' and Jermaine stepped in behind the glass. He briefly glanced over in our direction. I'm sure he was a little surprised at the number of people who were there to support him. I could see the look of embarrassment on his face as he stood in silence behind the glass as the Crown Attorney spoke.

I sat quietly in the back of the courtroom as the charges against Jermaine were read aloud in open court for the record. The court clerk began: "trafficking person exercise control, financial benefit from trafficking persons, exercise control of persons for prostitution, assault." The list went on, totaling ten separate charges. I couldn't allow myself to listen any further.

As the clerk continued, I took a deep breath and went to a happier place in my head to when Jermaine was a young child. The Crown Attorney then went on to describe Jermaine as a monster and a danger to the community, a person I knew nothing of. In fact, I barely recognized who she was speaking about. I watched Kelly as she too, tried to hold her composure. Kelly and I briefly held hands in support of each other and sat emotionless on the hard wooden bench. I felt her pain and could only imagine what her parents were thinking as they too sat and listened. I was horrified at the sight of all the other people in the body of the court as they too listened to the charges being read. What were they thinking? I'm sure they were sitting there judging my baby not knowing the person I knew.

Although the Crown Attorney and Cathy had already agreed that Jermaine would be released on bail, the conditions were strict, lengthy and significant including surety in the amount of $25,000.

Cathy assured the judge that there were several persons in the body of the court, including his mother, who were willing to guarantee Jermaine's surety and take responsibility for him should he see fit to grant her petition for bail.

As Kelly's parents were to be the main sureties, they were called to the stand one at a time to confirm their willingness and ability to act as Jermaine's surety and to confirm that they completely understood their role and responsibilities. I sat in awe as these virtual strangers swore under oath to not only guarantee an excessive amount of money but also to ensure that Jermaine followed whatever conditions were set out in the bail order should it be granted.

"Elaine Murdock!" Oh hell no, she's not calling me to the stand. I shook as I stood to my feet and approached the podium.

"Do you swear to tell the truth, the whole truth and nothing but the truth, so help you God?"

"I do," I responded as I held my hand on the Bible.

"Please state your name for the court spelling your last name." "Elaine Murdock .... E L A I N E M U R D O C K."

"Please be seated".

I sat nervously on the chair as Cathy approached me. "What is your relation to Jermaine Charles?"

"I'm his mother"

She then went on to verify that I was willing to be one of Jermaine's sureties, share responsibility for his release, ensure that he abided by the conditions as set out in his bail and also that I understood my responsibility to contact the court should he fail to do so. I agreed. The court clerk vigorously recorded the proceedings as we spoke.

Cathy then asked me about my place of employment. Something I was seriously hoping she wouldn't do. I guess it was somewhat obvious as I was still in uniform. I guess she thought it made me more credible in the eyes of the court. To me, it only reinforced my inability to properly steer my own child away from the court system given my work in Youth Justice.

"Thank you, Ms. Murdock. You may step down."

Without hesitation, I quickly stepped down and returned to my seat. I fought back the tears and prayed that it was enough for the judge to agree to bail. A few minutes later the judge addressed Jermaine, informing him that he would be released on bail as he was satisfied with the testimony of his sureties. He then proceeded to read out the conditions of his release which included a curfew and no use of a cellphone amongst others. The Judge confirmed that Jermaine understood the consequences should he fail to abide by them, for the record. Jermaine agreed and confirmed his understanding. He was then led out of the 'prisoner's box' and disappeared through the door to my left along with the two court officers.

"Now we wait," said Cathy. "Wait for the bail papers to be sent to the Justice of the Peace downstairs." Tears of relief slowly welled up in my eyes. "Cathy, thank you! Thank you!" I said as we all left the courtroom. A few short minutes later we arrived at the Justice of the Peace office and awaited the arrival of Jermaine's bail papers. "It may be a few hours" Cathy stated. "I have another matter to attend to. Take care. Please tell Jermaine that I will speak with him during the week." And with that she was gone.

We waited in virtual silence as I'm sure everyone was digesting the occurrences of the morning and what they had just heard. Almost three hours later and after swearing to the Justice of the Peace to diligently carry out our responsibilities as sureties, Jermaine's bail papers were signed and then copied for each of us. We then waited impatiently for almost another hour before Jermaine was brought upstairs from the holding cells. When he finally emerged through the doors, my face lit up like a Christmas tree and I quickly glanced down to make sure he wasn't still in handcuffs which also confirmed that this was really happening. I can't remember a time when I was happier to see him walk through a door other than the day I picked him up from his grandparent's home following my custody victory.

It was a small victory, but a victory nonetheless. At that point, I had to take what I could get. I did so with gratitude, not only to the court but to Kelly's parents to whom I would be forever indebted.

I left the court that day hand in hand with my prince as his new guardian angels followed behind. I held him close and then kissed him goodbye as he got into Kelly's vehicle. I embraced both Kelly's parents, thanking them for their unbelievable gesture and support, and then watched as they pulled out of the parking lot. David Jr. agreed to give me a drive home as I had totally forgotten that I did not have my car. We walked in silence to his vehicle and I climbed in feeling numb. I sat emotionless as he drove, thinking of where I had gone wrong. What could I have done differently, and what I would do if any of this was actually true. I stopped myself before heading down that road because I needed to believe in Jermaine's innocence; I wanted to revel in our recent victory a little longer.

As soon as we hit the road, I called Yvonne to tell her that Jermaine was on his way home. We didn't speak much of the charges as I had blocked out most of that information. Deep down I knew I would eventually have to come to terms with the accusations, but that was not the time. I needed to hang on to our victory just a little longer.

The Fall Out

Sometimes blind-faith is all we have
to go with.

When the phone unexpectedly rings in the middle of the night, you automatically know that it's not good news.

As I laid in bed to settle for the night, I was startled by the ringing of the phone that seemed to echo through my body like a scream flying through an empty room. I quickly reached for the receiver not expecting anything good to come from answering that unexpected call.

"Mom, turn on the news! Turn on the news!" was all I heard from the hysterical voice on the other end of the line. I recognized the voice as Kelly, Jermaine's girlfriend. The horror in her voice scared me. "Jermaine's on television and his picture is all over the news and the internet!" she continued. I didn't hear what she said at first, or was it that I didn't want to believe what I had heard? I sat straight up in the bed like the rising dead, which was no easy task as lately I had been rolling on my side to get up out of the bed due to different aches and pains.

In total disbelief, I reluctantly reached for the remote control on the nightstand beside my bed and pushed the power button. I silently prayed that it wouldn't work. Of course, it did.

It seemed as if the television itself didn't want to reveal what I was about to see because it took what seemed like forever to turn on. The glow from the television lit up the bedroom like the rising sun. I slowly pushed the white 'channel up' button on the remote and then parked on the local news channel. I watched as the well-dressed news reporters recapped the top stories of the day. With each story, my confidence that it was a bad dream began to grow only to be shattered like a boulder smashing into a windshield. There it was in full vibrant colour, a not so flattering photo of my prince, now a grown man. In total shock, I thought, He looks so old. Not something you would think of as a normal first thought in that circumstance, but the mind is a funny thing when it's trying to protect you.

The news caption read; "28-year-old man faces charges after police say woman was forced into sex trade" I didn't really hear anything else although his lips continued to move. I just stared at the photograph, or should I say mug shot, and pictured my prince as a toddler.

My body went numb. My words stuck in my throat. Too mortified for tears, I rapidly pushed on the white channel button moving from channel to channel hoping that what I was seeing was a mirage or just a nightmare. I quickly realized that it was neither as each channel repeated the same information, some alleging up to ten different charges against him. My heart sank to the pit of my stomach and the tears slowly began to roll down my face, rapidly increasing into what could only be described as a gushing fire hydrant.

As I crumpled onto the bedroom floor now in full blown inconsolable hysteria all I could think was; What is wrong with these people plastering innocent people's pictures all over the place like that? There is no way my baby is capable of that. No way. That was not how I raised him. He was raised by a single mother, surely he has more respect for women than that.

Then that very familiar but uncontrollable feeling of failure consumed every fibre of my being. What did I do so wrong? How could I have failed him so profoundly? Guilty or not, I obviously went wrong somewhere along the line. Suddenly fear set in which quickly grew to absolute terror as his two younger siblings, now teenagers, flashed into my mind. How do I tell his siblings? Especially his sister. What will they think? How will they handle this? How will this affect them? How will they manage at school once their friends and others hear the news? (We all know how mean kids can be.) The questions kept slamming into the side of my head, resulting in a massive headache.

How do you sit your teenagers down and tell them that their brother, whom they look up to, has been criminally charged with anything, never mind something like that? I had withheld Jermaine's past encounters with the law from them out of fear that they would judge him and see him differently ruining the incredible bond they all shared. I had very little time before I needed to speak with them. Social media travels at the speed of light and the last thing I wanted was for them to see this on television, the internet or through a friend's text message.

I mustered up all the energy I could and drew myself up off

the bedroom floor, wiped the tears and mucus from my face, and summoned them out of their bedrooms and into the living room. Their sleepy little faces had a tone of frustration and confusion all over them. After all, why was I dragging them out of bed at this time of the night?

We sat down on the grey sectional in the living room, one on each side of me. Then I just blurted it out, there was no other way. "Jermaine was arrested on Human Trafficking charges," I said. "It's on the news and I wanted you guys to hear it from me first." I could see the tears start to well up in Nicole's eyes. I drew her close and held her in my arms. Anthony simply withheld any emotions as I went on to explain what 'Human Trafficking" was and asked if they had any questions. "I know that he didn't do it, mommy, everything is going to be ok," Nicole said, triggering my endless stream of tears once again.

The next few minutes were spent searching the internet to see how much was already out there. It was everywhere! I couldn't believe it. In a matter of hours, news had spread to every news channel and several social media sites. Anthony simply got up from the sofa and returned to his room. He was never much of a talker and I assumed he needed to sort through this on his own.

Anger slowly replaced my tears as I thought of Jermaine's innocence and how the internet is forever. How will he ever be able to move forward with his life once the truth of his innocence comes to light and he is cleared of all these charges? I'm sure no one is going to go on the internet and say "oops it wasn't him! Sorry for ruining his life and the lives of those around him." Apologies never make the news headlines or get hits/likes on social media.

Should it even be allowed? Should your name and photo be plastered all over the internet when you are simply accused but not yet convicted of a crime? Having worked in the justice system for over 20 years, I am forever conflicted with the answer to that question as I've seen the positive outcomes as well as the devastation this can cause once the accused is proven to be innocent. The damage to reputation, self and family are irrevocable. The fallout is everywhere and very few people, if any, stay around to help clean up the mess. Families fall apart; parents' relationships end. The financial strain on some families is insurmountable. The emotional toll is immeasurable and often goes unrecognized until it manifests in unexpected ways months or even years later.

As the night turned into day, the phone began to ring off the hook. Family members and friends with questions and statements of concern and disbelief called one after the other. Most offering their support but some feeding their need for drama. My cell phone began to vibrate across the kitchen counter as the number of text messages and BBM's exploded. I could hear the kids' phones going off as well and I just knew that the news had reached their friends, and those who knew them best had put the pieces together.

They seemed to be handling it well through their unwavering confidence in their brothers' innocence. Me, I didn't have that luxury. I had to hope for the best and prepare myself for the worst. The 'what ifs' began:' What if I can't fix this? What if it's true? What if he's found guilty? What if he has to go to jail? How will I survive? How will his brother and sister cope? The answers to these questions seemed unattainable. My faith in him was all I had left so with that, I braced myself for the fallout.

My return to work was another dreaded event as I feared that my peers and others that I worked with had also seen the news reports. Even more frightening was the thought that the youth at work had seen it. How do I claim to have the ability and desire to help them turn their lives around when I couldn't do the same for my own son?

That morning, I reluctantly reported to work and immediately met with my Deputy to inform her of the situation. I requested some flexibility in my approved time off so that I could be there for Jermaine during his court appearances. Francis was amazing. She listened as I revealed only as much information as I needed to. She watched and consoled me as I literally broke down in her office again, overwhelmed by feelings of fear, failure and hopelessness. I cried inconsolably, losing all control of my emotions right there in front of a literal stranger. She offered her support, and then told me that she would have to inform the Youth Centre Administrator but strictly on a need to know basis.

The Search for theTruth

*There's my story, your story and the
truth that lies somewhere in between.*

In mid-August 2014, I again made the grueling trip to Finch Court. This time Jermaine was to appear in court to be provided with his disclosure. This court document contains all information regarding the charges being brought against the accused, including statements from the alleged victim and witnesses if applicable.

December 2014, it was back to court, for a variation on Jermaine's bail conditions. Cathy had petitioned the court for a change to Jermaine's curfew condition which stated that he was not permitted outside between the hours of 6:00pm and 7:00am, without the accompaniment of one of his surety. Cathy argued to have the condition removed or at the very least amended in order to allow Jermaine to meet the requirements of his employment. The Crown Attorney vigorously argued against this request, however, in the end she agreed to amend the condition to "between the hours of 9:00pm to 7:00am." Another small victory. I hoped that it was a sign of others to come with the ultimate victory being dismissal of all charges.

A chilly morning in September 2015, I awoke to the screeching sound of my alarm. It had been an extremely restless night as that day's court appearance was a crucial one. That was the day that the details of the allegation were heard directly from the alleged victim. I sprung out of the bed, flew into the shower and threw on the clothes I had a laid out the night before.

As I dressed, I secretly hoped and prayed that it would be the last time I would have to return to the place I had slowly grown a strong hatred for, that there would be no victim on the stand, and we would find out that there in fact, was no victim because the whole thing was all a big lie.

I got into the car and headed to the courthouse. I was trying desperately not to think of what I might hear yet I could not stop my brain from working overtime. As a mother, I knew that no matter what I heard it would not change my love for Jermaine. I knew that I had to gather all my strength in order to stand strong by his side.

The drive was surprisingly quick, given that it was rush hour. It's probably because I really didn't want to get there, I thought. I pulled into the parking lot and realized that I was the first to arrive because I didn't see Jermaine, Kelly or her parents. I immediately called Kelly wondering if I had gotten the court date wrong. After three rings, Kelly answered the phone stating that they were on their way and would be there shortly. For the next 10 minutes, I sat in the car with the music blaring on the stereo. That was my way of warding off the anxiety I was beginning to feel. The butterflies were having a field day in my stomach and nausea was beginning to set up shop.

Kelly's large black SUV pulled into a parking space several cars over from where I sat in my car. It's now or never, I thought as I reluctantly got out of my vehicle. Oh, stop it! She's not going to be here because there's nothing to tell, I convinced myself. After a short greeting in the parking lot, Jermaine, Kelly, her parents and I headed into the courthouse for what we were hoping was the last time.

Into the drab looking building, through the metal detectors and down the corridor we shuffled. Cathy was waiting for us in front of courtroom 208, a number I was becoming a little too familiar with. We all sat while she spoke with Jermaine, informing him of what to expect when he entered the courtroom. She also verified that the alleged victim would be taking the stand. Her words shattered my hopes like a fist hitting a mirror and I fought to hold the contents of my breakfast down.

A few minutes later, we were all asked to enter the courtroom and take a seat. We sat in the back of the room as we did in the past and awaited the judge's entrance. Cathy immediately appeared engrossed in a conversation with the Crown. I could tell something was going on because Cathy didn't look happy. "ALLLL RISE!" We all stood as required. The judge entered the courtroom in his black robe with white color and took his seat. "You may be seated." We sat like trained dogs reacting to a command. The Crown immediately began to inform the judge of concerns regarding the alleged victim's testimony. She informed the judge that the alleged victim was "afraid of the accused" and asked the court to allow the introduction of some type of precaution to ensure the alleged victims safety in the courtroom. Are you kidding me!? Security in the courtroom and in the building isn't enough? What does she think he's going to do to her in a courtroom packed with people?

The Crown went on to request that a screen be used which would block Jermaine's view of alleged victim while she testified. Cathy adamantly opposed, describing this measure as excessive and unnecessary, but to no avail. The judge ordered a brief recess while the screen was located and set up in the courtroom. I can't believe this. They're treating him like he's Hannibal Lecter or something. Several minutes later a small screen, designed to allow the alleged victim to see the accused while blocking the accused view of them, was brought into the courtroom and set up on the podium from where the alleged victim would testify. Jermaine was instructed to move his chair slightly and to look in the other direction while the alleged victim entered the courtroom. Really?!

A young lady of small stature with light blond hair, a pale complexion and dark glasses entered the room from behind a door to our left and took her place behind the screened podium. The Crown then began. After stating her name for the record, the alleged victim proceeded to recount her version of the events. We all sat quietly as she gave details of her employment as a dancer and a prostitute and of her supposed relationship with Jermaine. She spoke in detail of the alleged events which eventually led her to contact the police. Every bone in my body wanted to get up and leave, but I didn't want to give Jermaine or the Court the wrong impression. So I sat and again tried to tune out as much as possible as she spoke in order to preserve my sanity and keep my emotions in check. Although I tried, I could not keep my tears at bay. They slowly crept down my cheeks quicker than I could wipe them away as I tried to make sense of her words.

Kelly and her parents again sat silently next to me. Kelly's show of strength was impressive given the alleged victims testimony. She showed very little response. Was it due to her unwavering belief in Jermaine or had she also tuned out in order to protect herself?

After nearly five hours of testimony from the alleged victim, court was adjourned. A piece of me knew that there had to be some truth to what I had just heard. How much? I dared not venture to guess.

Jermaine's next court date was set for a few months later. We exited the courtroom much as we entered: In silence. I left with more questions than answers and could only pray that the real truth would soon be revealed.

It has now been two long years since this was first brought before the court, with still no resolution in sight. Now, I share my story with others on a similar journey, continue to pray, to grow, to learn and most of all to survive.

Falling Back on Faith

Time on your krnees is always time
well spent.

I have always considered myself a spiritual person, although I don't attend church on a regular basis. I believe that God has a plan and a purpose for us all, although we may not always understand it.

He does seem to have quite the sense of humour though. As He tends to reveal his plan in pieces much like a gig-saw puzzle. Then just for kicks, He leaves out one important piece, waiting for us to help ourselves. That's the piece that forces us to think, to grow in ourselves and in our faith.

That's the piece that gets us moving in one of two directions. Away from His grace or into His favour.

I must confess that I spent a lot of time moving away from His grace over the years but I slowly began to find my way back. A journey that is still quite rocky for the most part but steady nonetheless. I've learned to pray again and to give thanks no matter how small I may think the favour. In Him, I've found great strength.

I will say that, my latest journey with Jermaine helped to rekindle my faith and brought me crashing to my knees. It was a force I had never felt before. A compulsion to seek His guidance. Someone must have the answers I seek. It became more obvious as the time passed that I had just been looking in the wrong places. I was lost in absolute darkness, consumed by guilt having failed everyone so profoundly. I began to question my very existence. What's my purpose? Why had He entrusted me, not once but three times with His greatest gift of all, the gift of motherhood? I was sure that I was nowhere close to deserving or worthy of this gift and the proof was right there for all to see.

Tears began to well up in my eyes as thoughts of unworthiness overwhelmed my brain when, without hesitation He intervened. Like someone turning on a light switch, I realized that I wasn't alone! He was always there, all I had to do was believe and have the strength to ask Him for guidance. At that moment, I also realized that He had already answered my prayers. He had blessed me with his messengers who in a short period of time had already impacted my life as no one ever had.

Several years prior I had been fortunate enough to be introduced to the most amazing family of God I have ever met. Pastor Jeff Wallace, Mother Wallace, his son Pastor Owen Wallace and his faithful wife, Francine. This family is truly infectious with their faith and love for all those around them.

Pastor Jeff Wallace stood not much more than 5'5" tall, with a smooth brown complexion, bald head and stalky frame, and the most infectious smile you would ever come across. Mother Wallace was the perfect match for him. She stood not much more than 5'4", and she too had a smooth chocolate brown complexion, black hair and a radiant smile. Owen, a handsome young man standing about 6', also sporting a bald head and a medium build his wife Francine who can only be described as beautiful, inside and out. 5'8" or so, slim build, beautiful brown complexion and shoulder length black hair.

They automatically became an extension of my family and welcomed me with open arms every time we met. They made my journey back to faith an easy one and taught me to believe even when I felt that all hope was gone.

Although I attended church sporadically they had a way of making me feel as though we had seen each other only minutes ago. Their unconditional love and support gave me a feeling of belonging. Pastor Owen was particularly supportive, checking in on me regularly. His sincerity was refreshing and I knew that no matter what it was, he would be there to help me maneuver through the obstacles. He was like my guardian angel. If you believe in that kind of thing.

Jermaine's last charge took all I had left. I was consumed with guilt and felt more lost than I ever had.

At my lowest point, I picked up the phone and messaged Pastor Owen that I needed to speak with him. Without hesitation, he called and informed me that he could come by my home later that day.

That evening, Pastor Owen arrived at my home and greeted me with a supportive embraced. "What's going on Elaine?" We sat down in the living room in silence as I tried to pull myself together. I had no idea where to start. After all, how do you tell your pastor that your child was charged with human trafficking amongst other charges? Despite knowing that there would be no judgment or blame I was so embarrassed and ashamed that all I could do was cry. Through the tears I began to tell Pastor Owen about Jermaine's situation, and my overwhelming feelings of guilt and shame, and the paralyzing fear that consumed me when I dared to think of a possible finding of guilt and incarceration.

He listened with compassion and assured me that the truth would come to light and that things would be as they should. As simple as that sounds, it was extremely comforting. My faith was once again renewed that day and I am truly thankful for his presence in my life. Because of him, I began to look deep for my true inner strength but also realized that I would have to accept my limitations and leave the rest to God. I realized that I was not alone on this journey and that I had not only the strength but the ability and responsibility to help others as they too walk along this path.

That day left me with a new focus and determination to not only see Jermaine through his ordeal while focusing on my own self-preservation with the understanding that "God doesn't give us more than we can handle;" but determined to help others also on this journey. As I began to speak of my struggles with others, I quickly realized that by sharing my story, I wasn't just on a path to healing but was helping others as well. I slowly came to terms with the fact that on this journey, the lesson is not only Jermaine's but mine as well. It was time to examine the past, extract the lessons learned, embrace my present and plan for the future. It was time to pull myself up and focus on my own self-healing and allow the good Lord to guide my way.

From Trials to Triumph

Every test truly makes us stronger.
The key is to share that strength with
others still struggling to make their
way.

For the next week, I tried desperately not to spiral into a deep depression again. I knew that what I was feeling wasn't something I could ignore or go through on my own. My first thought was to call my family doctor. What on earth was I going to say to him this time? I really had no clue. How could I get him to understand how I was truly feeling? How could someone like him, who clearly would have no idea where I was coming from help me? Not this time. Not with this.

It was a Tuesday morning when I picked up the phone, dialed the phone number for his office and cried as it began to ring. By the time Jan picked up on the other end, I was clearly distraught and could barely speak. This time, her cheery voice on the other end of the line did nothing to lift my spirits. I explained to her that I was having an extremely hard time holding it together and needed to see Dr. Patrick again. He was the psychiatrist I had seen many years prior. She explained that since it had been so long since I had seen Dr. Patrick, I would need a referral and that it would possibly be months before I would get an appointment. I was devastated. I felt like she too had just stabbed me in the stomach. She went on to tell me that if things got really bad, I was to go to the nearest emergency department as I would receive an immediate referral there along with support and treatment if needed.

A lot of help that was. Now what? I tried to speak with my sisters but could only give them a glimpse of what was truly going on because they too couldn't begin to understand how I felt because they had never been there. I was certain that this type of fear, hopelessness and despair could only be understood by someone who had been there. I was convinced that I would be judged and seen as the failure as none of their children had taken them down this path.

Exposure of weakness is a difficult thing for anyone to deal with because we all like to believe that we are strong and alone we can deal with anything that comes our way. But this, this was different, it's nothing you can ever really prepare for. It's something that usually blindsides you when you come to the realization that your life is out there for all to judge, and judge they will. I found myself deceiving those around me, as I was too ashamed and embarrassed, not only of the actions of my own children but especially of my inability to be the 'perfect mother' who raised the 'perfect children.' I was never good with failure and this was failure on the grandest scale.

Family breakdown is another hard reality when family members are thrust into the limelight and unfairly judged due only to their relation. I was lucky. My family and friends stood by my side, at least, the ones I chose to tell. To this day my mother is unaware of her grandchildren's struggle with the law. Turning to friends was out of the question as I was too ashamed to share the depth of my weakness and the feelings of helplessness. My partner watched helplessly as I withdrew from him and the world.

I lived in constant fear that someone else would find out the truth and dreaded those casual conversations in social circles which almost always lead to questions like: How are the kids? What are they doing now? I struggled to find answers that wouldn't raise eyebrows bringing further judgement of my children and myself. Most of the time I just averted the questions by deflection or simply said: "They're fine, you know teenagers, they're doing their own thing" and then quickly changed the subject.

I couldn't return to work due to my inability to control my emotional outbursts. How could I be of any use to someone else's child when I couldn't even keep my own children from walking down this path. I felt as though I was not only an unfit parent but also incapable of doing the job I loved. I began to have thoughts of paranoia convinced that the system that I had dedicated my entire adult life to serving was now out to destroy me and my children. Just the thought of seeing a police officer, never mind having to deal with them at work, was enough to overwhelm me with feelings of anger and embarrassment. My workplace became intolerable and I was forced to remove myself from that environment and take some time to gather myself and refocus. I was fortunate enough to be reassigned to another area of my job on a temporary basis, which took me out of the facility and removed the expectation of direct contact with the youth and law enforcement. I clearly needed help. More than a job change could provide. So I went on the hunt for some sort of support. There had to be something out there. Prayer served its purpose but as they say "God helps those who help themselves."

I turned to the Internet in search of assistance. Surely, I wasn't the only parent going through this. That much I knew for a fact as I had spoken with an endless number of parents over the years, in the course of my work. There had to be some kind of support group, helpline or something out there specific to my situation. Not only was I devastated to discover that there was nothing in my area but disgusted knowing what that meant for endless number of parents in my position and those still to come. So I continued to browse, widening my search, this time finding several support groups for children whose parents were in custody. After what seemed like hours of searching I came across one program that supported parents with children in custody, located in New York City, which was no longer in existence I must add. Really???!!!!

Now fueled by anger, I dug deeper and dove back into the search, frantically imputing any keywords I could think of. My relentless search turned up some Federal groups for families of "lifers" and others serving time but nothing specific to my need. It was, however, great to see so many supports for youth with parents in custody and various other supports for youth in general.

However, what about the families and guardians of youth and young adults in conflict with the law? They too become victims of the system and are in need of support. For those families, the journey begins the minute they become aware of their child's conflict with the law. This usually catches them totally off guard and unprepared for the challenges of maneuvering through the complex legal system. It is at that point that the circumstances begin to take its toll. Families are left in the aftermath of these life-changing ordeals in which they have to bear not only the emotional impact, financial burden, and alienation from friends and other family members, but also the task of caring for the immediate family.

In total annoyance, I slammed the laptop closed so hard that the table shook. Then I had a good cry. You know the type of cry that comes from total frustration, anger, and fear? Somehow those are the ones that hit you deep in your soul and flush out some form of clarity.

It was then that I realized that I had a responsibility to myself, my children and others to stand up and give thanks for my many blessings. I also had the responsibility to use the lessons learned from my many challenges to help others through the tunnel and into the light of their own redemption and healing. In doing so, I too would find my way. That realization led me to the next chapter of my life.

For days, all I could think of was how I was going to turn my many trials into triumph. What was my lesson in all this? How was I going to make the best of this nightmare and ultimately help others do the same? Over the next few days, I discussed my idea of starting a support group for parents of youth in conflict with the law with Pastor Owen and a few of my colleagues at work. I wanted to hear their feed-back and further wanted to determine if they were aware of any such support groups of this kind. The response was always the same. "This is a great idea, Elaine. Something that is in great need and would help so many."

I knew that I no longer walked alone, yet countless others were truly struggling without the benefit of any support. One of the most devastating feelings is that of isolation with nowhere to turn. TWRS - Together We R Strong was born that night out of desperation and necessity. So I set out to launch a support group for parents/guardians of youth in conflict with the law. This group would offer parents/guardians support in the form of open, confidential conversation with others in similar situations. It would offer parents/guardians the opportunity to share their stories and draw on each other's strengths. The goal is for families to support each other as they move through the justice system alongside their children, dealing with the many stresses they will face along that path. TWRS – Together We R Strong would encourage others to step out from the shadows, to speak of their struggles and to move Beyond the Shame onto a path of self-healing.

Over the next few weeks, I developed the concept, designed flyers, brochures, promotional postcards and launched a website.

With the unwavering support of my children, TWRS - Together We R Strong was officially launched in November of 2014. I realize that many are still too ashamed to speak of their ordeal publicly so with this understanding, I continue to stand strong in my commitment to offer this support. I hope that one day we will all be accepting of everyone and empathetic to their struggles. We all deserve the space to heal with freedom from judgment, alienation and ridicule. To this end, I continue to share my story and speak with others about their struggles knowing that the path to healing is neither easy nor short for any of us.

Tying it all up

As the words started to pour out onto the pages as easily as pouring my morning cup of tea, I quickly came to realize that although this started as a therapeutic exercise for me I wasn't just writing this for myself but for all those who are silenced by their shame and trapped under the weight of their guilt.

It is my hope that until you are ready and able to free yourself from your self-imposed prison, reading my story will serve as inspiration and comfort. You did not fail, you will survive and together we are strong. We no longer have to be the invisible victims of circumstances hiding Beyond the Shame.

We are proud, strong and resilient human beings who have walked and are still walking an incredible journey of growth, change, acceptance and healing.

I've finally learned that my children's actions are not a reflection of who I am but rather the propensity of the human brain to make decisions for itself, sometimes without the benefit of knowledge and/ or consequence. When times got really tough, Nicole was my solace. She was my constant reminder that I did not totally fail my children. She persevered through this journey standing by her brother's side with unconditional love and grace. She is now in University pursuing a degree in Psychology. Anthony to date, has not incurred any further charges and continues his journey of personal growth. I pray that he finds his true strengths along the way. It has been more than two years since I began my last journey by Jermaine's side with still no resolution or end in sight. So I continue to pray and share my story as we all prepare for the challenges and victories ahead.

To date, although I continue in search of that one thing that I could and/or should have done differently, that would have changed the course of my children's lives and subsequently mine, it is no longer my driving force. The guilt and shame still exist but it is minimal and no longer paralyzing. It now pushes me to grow and become stronger in my commitment to help others as they embark on a similar journey with their children.

Although there were many lessons along the way and I continue to learn from my experiences, I would like to share the most helpful lessons I learned on this voyage.

Regardless of your life's path, I hope these tips will help you find peace.

Tips for Survival

1. Take care of yourself – The most important thing you can do for your loved one is to take care of yourself; physically, emotionally and spiritually. It will take all the strengths you have to get through this type of ordeal and they will also rely on your strength. Seek counseling, join the gym. Make yourself a priority even when everything in you is telling you otherwise. Seek out support groups in your community and/or speak to someone you trust.

2. Be non-judgemental - As hard as this sounds judgment from you is the last thing your child needs. No matter how hard you try, you will never be able to understand the circumstances which led them to where they are. The choices they face every day are unimaginable. Their world can be confusing, intimidating and sometimes frightening and survival is sometimes there driving factor. Remember you are not their only influence as hard as you may try.

3. Show empathy and compassion - Listen with compassion and empathy. It's not easy for them to express themselves. Although you may not understand their reasoning or explanation, take comfort in the fact that they're speaking at all.

4. Be supportive - Be there for them. No matter how small the gesture, it means more to them than they will let on. Your presence at court, at lawyer visits, etc. is paramount. Even when they say they don't need you there, take it from me, they do.

5. Educate yourself - Maneuvering through the justice system is not an easy task. The more you know, the better prepared you will be to support your loved one. Ask questions; Do your research online or otherwise. A lot of lawyers offer free consultations online and in person and will generally answer your questions and guide you in the right direction. Seek out those in similar situations, as they too can be a great resource. Maintain regular contact with their lawyer in regards to what happens next and/or what can be expected.

6. Communicate your feelings - Speak with those around you. Let them know how you are affected by this and what you need. The emotional price tag can be a large one. Untreated stress and emotional strain can be costly when ignored and will manifest in many different ways over time.

7. Love unconditionally - Regardless of their choices and situation, they are still your children, your loved ones, and this is the time to love them even more. Although you do not condone their situation, now is when they will need you more than ever. A mother's love never dies.

8. Share your experience and support others - It is through the support of others in similar situations that you will find your greatest strength. Remember you are not alone. There are many who have taken this journey before you, who are now on a similar journey of their own, and there will be many others to follow.

9. Stay positive - One of the hardest things to do is to avoid thinking of the worst-case scenario. The 'what if's'. They are usually the cause of great emotional turmoil and a waste of energy that can be better utilized. Celebrate the small victories and embrace the lessons learned along the way knowing that things may not always go your way.

10. Prepare - Although there is no real way to prepare for something like this, always hope for the best but prepare for the worse as they say. Speak with other family members about the situation and possible outcomes. Be as forthcoming as possible (age appropriate) being careful not to imply guilt when unknown. Communicate with employers around possible flexibility in work schedules and other accommodations as needed. Financial costs can sneak up on you and catch you off guard. Communicate regularly with lawyers around legal fees or apply for Legal Aid. Seek emotional and spiritual support for all involved.

Last but not least:

11. Forgive yourself – Self-blame and self-doubt will only lead to self-destruction. Have faith that you did the best you could with the knowledge and tools you had at the time. Let go of the "if only I hads." You can no more control others choices than you can the weather.

Beyond the Shame lies immeasurable strength!

You are not alone!!

For more information about TWRS – Together We R Strong
Visit and/or contact us at: Website: www.twrstrong.com

Twitter: @TWRStrong

Facebook: www.facebook.com\twrstrong

Email: twrstrong@gmail.com

Author Bio

M.E. Murdock is a divorced mother of three amazing and distinctly unique children. She has dedicated more than 20 years to working with adults and youth in conflict with the law. By providing support, guidance and sometimes good old fashion honesty she has helped countless number of youth to turn their lives around by helping them to recognize their worth and potential. She has also supported an increasing number of families as they deal with the devastating effects of their child's incarceration. She has witnessed first-hand, what a child's incarceration can do, not only to the child, but to their families. M.E. Murdock has championed through many life challenges including her own children's walk on the wrong side of the law. She's the founder of TWRS - Together We R Strong, a support group for parents of youth in conflict with the law. TWRS - Together We R Strong provides the opportunity for parents to come together, share experiences and support each other through open, confidential conversation.

Learn more at: www.twrstrong.com

Made in the USA
Columbia, SC
20 September 2017